Julian Nava

My Mexican-American Journey

Julian Nava

My Mexican-American Journey

Julian Nava

Foreword by Henry A. J. Ramos

Arte Público Press
Houston, Texas

This volume is made possible through grants from the Charles Stewart Mott Foundation, the Ewing Marion Kauffman Foundation, the Rockefeller Foundation, and the City of Houston through The Cultural Arts Council of Houston, Harris County.

Recovering the past, creating the future

Arte Público Press
University of Houston
452 Cullen Performance Hall
Houston, Texas 77204-2004

Cover design by James Brisson

Nava, Julian, 1927–.
Julian Nava: My Mexican-American journey / Julian Nava; Foreword by Henry A. J. Ramos.
p. cm.
Summary: Julian Nava recounts his rise from a childhood in the barrio to become the first Mexican American to serve as United States Ambassador to Mexico.
ISBN 1-55885-364-2 (clothbound : alk. paper)
ISBN 1-55885-351-0 (paperback)
1. Nava, Julian, 1927—Juvenile literature 2. Mexican Americans—Biography—Juvenile literature. 3. Statesmen—United States—Biography—Juvenile literature. 4. Educators—United States—Biography—Juvenile literature. 5. Civil rights workers—United States—Biography—Juvenile literature. 6. Mexican Americans—United States—Biography—Juvenile literature. 7. Mexican Americans—Politics and government—20th century—Juvenile literature. 8. Mexican Americans—Education—Juvenile literature. [1. Nava, Julian, 1927– 2. Statesmen. 3. Mexican Americans—Biography.] I. Title.
E184.M5 N288 2002
370′.92—dc21 2001058993
[B] CIP

♾ The paper used in this publication meets the requirements of the American National Standard for Information Sciences—Permanence of Paper for Printed Library Materials, ANSI Z39.48-1984.

2 3 4 5 6 7 8 9 0 1 10 9 8 7 6 5 4 3 2 1

Table of Contents

Dedication

This book is dedicated to my grandchildren, and theirs in time. I hope they have good teachers as I have had from Bridge Street School in the barrio to my professors at Harvard University that helped me learn how to learn on my own.

Foreword

The 1960s and 1970s produced historically significant gains for Hispanic elected and appointed officials, and by extension for historically disadvantaged Latino communities. After having been long denied meaningful opportunities in policy making prior to these years, Latinos of this era began to work for a new political consciousness informed largely by former World War II veterans from cities and states across the nation. Their work and evolution as public leaders helped to create a new backdrop and context for Latino public engagement, which ultimately enabled this new generation of policy advocates and practitioners to secure major reforms in U.S. law and custom. These reforms in turn helped to change the face of American politics, both in terms of its content and accessibility relative to Spanish-speaking communities. As a result, Latino leaders began to emerge for the first time during this era as significant local, statewide, national, and international policy practitioners. Latino legislative leaders, like Edward Roybal of Los Angeles, Henry B. González of Texas, Joseph Montoya and Manuel Luján of New Mexico, and Robert García of New York are examples of this major breakthrough in American politics.

One of the trailblazers of this modern Latino political movement was Dr. Julian Nava. A former navy airman and one of the first-ever Mexican-American graduates of Pomona College and Harvard University, Nava was elected to the Los Angeles Board of Education in 1967. He was the first Hispanic in contemporary times to sit on that important body, which is responsible for administering the nation's second-largest public school district. Later, in 1979, Nava was appointed by U.S. President Jimmy Carter to become the first (and still the only) Mexican American ever to serve as an American ambassador to Mexico. Both prior to and since these landmark accomplishments, Nava's life has been marked by other important distinctions, as well as moments of unique personal and historical poignancy that make him one of the most interesting figures of twentieth-century Latino politics. In many respects, Nava's life has tracked the U.S. Latino community's journey and experience of the past century, marked initially by squalor and institutional marginalization but ultimately characterized—through remarkable will, grace, and wisdom—by major societal accomplishments and contributions.

Nava's autobiography, chronicled in the pages that follow here, reflects the epic journey and candid (if at times controversial) observations and opinions of an especially important figure in modern Mexican-American political life. His journey takes him from places as varied as the streets of East Los Angeles to the Great Wall of China, from Harvard Yard to Fidel Castro's Cuba, from the small Mexican village of Tepetongo, Zacatecas, Mexico, where his family's odyssey began, to the icy plains of Siberia. Nava's story covers the struggles of his impoverished immigrant family during his Depression-era childhood, his call to military duty as a teenager during World War II, his unusually impressive higher educational achievements and postdoctoral work focused on (and in) Latin America and Spain, and his unlikely rise to political leadership during one of the stormiest periods in American educational policy. Nava's memoir includes telling reflections on the nature of institutionalized racism in American society and politics, the depth of graft and misdealing in public life, and the personal price of leading with integrity.

In reading Nava's reflections on his extraordinary journey, one is struck by the unusual breadth of his cultural range, the multiplicity and selflessness of his life pursuits, and the irrepressible centrality of his commitment to family, friends, and certain core values. One is impressed as well by Nava's intellectual honesty, his straightforward inclination to speak his notion of truth, and his deep commitment to civility (even in the face of real conflict). Men like Nava are increasingly difficult to find in today's world, one senses, especially in the world of public leadership.

When I was growing up in Los Angeles and attending elementary and middle school, Julian Nava became president of the Los Angeles public school board. During these tumultuous years, I can attest to the fact that he oversaw one of the most significant shifts in the political landscape that our city's and the nation's public schools had ever witnessed. In the aftermath of major police-community conflicts involving African-American and Mexican-American residents of the nation's second largest city, and in the face of a controversial court order to desegregate the city's schools through imposed busing, Nava remained a voice of reason and calm in a time of real and imminent public discord.

Shortly thereafter, Nava was appointed to serve as the U.S. ambassador to Mexico, in a historical moment that ushered in a volatile new era in east-west and north-south relations—an era in which Mexico's role was particularly significant. During this sensitive period, Mexico emerged as a major producer of petroleum products shortly after a major embargo on Western exports by traditional Arab oil producing nations. Mexico also stood at the doorstep of growing U.S. concerns about problems associated with illegal immigration, drug trafficking, and regional terrorism. In an increasing number of cases, Mexico found itself greatly at odds with American policy and increasingly positioned to effectively challenge its neighbor to the north. Again, through the many conflicts created by these circumstances involving Mexican, American, and other world leaders, Nava served with unusual distinction, responsibility, and care.

Notwithstanding these significant contributions to the public good, his many groundbreaking educational achievements and numerous subsequent pursuits of note (including an unsuccessful effort to become the first modern Hispanic mayor of Los Angeles), Julian Nava remains largely unknown to many contemporary Americans, and especially younger Americans. The important story that he tells will help to change that, and should; for Nava's story is a remarkably American story that speaks to the inherent vision, talent, and skill of the nation's Latino people—too many of whom have been denied the opportunity to realize their full potential in American society. Nava's story is a reminder of what an extraordinary individual can accomplish in this nation, even when that success is deftly achieved not because of, but rather in spite of, prevailing public policies and practices.

Nava's story appears here in publication as part of an important new book series sponsored by Arte Público Press, with support from major private funding institutions, including the Charles Stewart Mott Foundation, the Ewing Marion Kauffman Foundation, and the Rockefeller Foundation. The series is intended to educate and inform American readers, and especially younger readers, about the many contributions of Latino leaders, civic institutions, and community movements to American civic culture since the end of World War II. By recounting these stories, we seek to encourage a stronger sense of the need for continuing efforts to promote social, economic, and political measures that help to accelerate Americans' appreciation of cultural diversity as an essential national asset. Indeed, the timing of this effort is critical, as we have recently begun to witness the evolution of Latinos as the nation's largest minority population. By the year 2050, it is anticipated that Latinos will constitute fully one-quarter of the American population. With such data and realities before us, it is more imperative than ever that Americans of all backgrounds come to better understand the histories of our expanding national Latino population, as well as the many positive roles Hispanic people have played and will continue to play in advancing America's promise.

The life story of Dr. Julian Nava will inspire readers of all backgrounds to better comprehend and appreciate these concepts and their growing importance in our national life and discourse. It is our great pleasure and honor, therefore, to offer *Julian Nava: My Mexican-American Journey* as a leading entry in our series.

Henry A. J. Ramos
Executive Editor
Hispanic Civil Rights Series

Chapter 1

My Mexican Roots

Everything I am and how I think have been shaped by my Mexican roots. My mother told us about how she and our father came from two small, mountain towns in Zacatecas. Tepetongo and Susticacán were a day's walk apart, so it was not surprising that young Ruth Flores Casas did not know Julián Nava Carlos. They were to meet years later in the United States. Purely by chance, we know more about my mother's early life than my father's. However, Nava folks keep turning up since my name has been in the public media.

My mother's parents owned the general store in Tepetongo, as well as some land outside of town. As the only daughter, she was the darling of her parents and two brothers. Her parents selected her husband as was common in those days. She saw her future husband up close and spoke to him for the first time at the wedding ceremony.

I have been to the small chapel where my mother got married. I sat down on a worn pew and wondered about the customs of those days as the organist played medieval church music, just as he had for her wedding. The church organist was my cousin Jesús María Flores, and he loved to play the organ and sing the mass in Latin. My mother was not happy with her husband. Ventura was tall, good-looking, and a hard worker. He provided a large adobe house with a small orchard just outside of town. You can still see the old house and outdoor oven where she cooked and made tortillas from corn they grew. Ventura was a good man and provider, but he was very serious and harsh in his treatment of everyone. Like a good wife, my mother made the best of her situation because divorce was unheard of in those small towns. Her life evolved around her two sons, one of whom died as a child from a sickness that would easily be cured in a city.

Everyone in such small towns supported the president, Don Porfirio Díaz, who had governed Mexico for about thirty years by the turn of the century. People there were hardworking, self-sufficient, and conservative. Order and stability were the keys to a good life. Order and stability favored the rich and powerful, including foreigners. Díaz favored foreigners because he believed they brought new ideas and investments that would modernize Mexico. The country became more modern with banks, telephones, railroads, and new industries, but the vast majority of Mexicans gained little from all this. Gradually, the regime of Don Porfirio aroused increasing opposition, even among some of the wealthy people and writers on public affairs by 1910.

Mother was a natural storyteller, and I enjoyed her stories about the Mexican history she had lived through. She related how the Mexican Revolution of 1910 started from within, as Díaz supporters argued over who would succeed the "old man." Before long, other revolutionary groups rose among the poor. These groups wanted a complete change and not just a better working system. The years of terrible fighting broke out gradually when Don Porfirio left Mexico in disgust. Díaz was both sad and mad that his countrymen did not appreciate his service as president. He had given Mexico the first and most prosperous period in its history.

The revolution is fascinating on its own; however, it helps explain why I was born in California. Peaceful towns like Susticacán and Tepetongo were torn apart by fighting during the revolution. My mother told us about how roving bands of soldiers would ride into town by surprise. It made no difference if they were government *federales* or revolutionaries. They both did the same things. They took food, supplies, horses, money, and kidnapped women. In order to survive, these communities pretended to be on the side of whoever occupied the town for a week or so.

Although some young men volunteered to join one group or another, time after time the soldiers drafted men of fighting age by force. Pretty girls were in great danger of being kidnapped. Finding themselves stranded from home and family, the girls became caretakers for their soldiers and bore them children. In some cases, a girl would fall in love and willingly follow her man off to war. My mother told us about how families built false walls in their homes to hide boys and girls whenever the alarm was sounded. Young boys were assigned to sit on hilltops to spot cavalry dust approaching. Mountain towns like Susticacán and Tepetongo were never attacked; they were simply milked to death over the years. Before long, few men were available to do the everyday work. The loss of stored food and supplies threatened starvation before the next harvest. I never heard Mother or people in these towns say anything good about the revolution.

Ventura Muñatones decided to take his family away from all this. Mexican labor was valuable to the United States. After the First World War ended, no one bothered to count Mexicans crossing the border. Ventura, my mother, and their children left their farm in the care of relatives. El Salitral, as it is still called, soon broke down. Its stone-carved doorways and huge ceiling beams left evidence that it was once part of a large country home.

My father and his older brother abandoned Susticacán

for similar reasons. My dad was a well-read person and was a socialist, judging from some of the books we had at home. He favored the revolutionary cause, but in time the Navas must have seen that fighting made little sense, because one military group was no better than the other.

When my father settled in Los Angeles, he married and then divorced. I have always wondered if I have half-brothers somewhere. He owned part of a block in downtown Los Angeles, which was a pasture at that time but now has skyscrapers on it. He lost the property in the divorce, I guess. I would like to learn more about this part of his life, but the folks who could tell me are all dead now.

My mother's first husband, Ventura, died in the great flu epidemic of the twenties, leaving my mother a widow with a boy and a girl in a foreign country. Mexican families took care of their own, so Mother had assistance from relatives. *Zacatecanos* grouped together in the American barrios. In this manner, Mother met my father, who was a distant relative by marriage. I can see why Julián Nava was attracted to the young widow with two children. Throughout her life, Mother had a twinkle in her eyes and loved to sing, dance, and enjoy endless conversation. Father's older brother did not approve of my parents' marriage, I gather from family stories. As a child, I always wondered why we did not visit much with my uncle Lucío Nava. Lucío was a fine tailor and made clothes for movie actors. He owned some rental houses in a barrio called Maravilla and was better off financially than my father. The cousins did have contact with each other, however.

Chapter 2

My Early Barrio Memories

My memory starts when we lived in East Los Angeles in a neighborhood called Boyle Heights. Boyle Heights was like the United Nations because of all the immigrant children in school from different countries. I recall Italians, Japanese, Armenians, Russians, Mexicans, and Jews, to mention just a few. Americans, or Anglos as we called them, were there also, but they were a minority. We were Mexicans, and we called others by their nationality, like Armenians, Russians, or Italians, because that was what they were to us. The first house I remember living in was on Lord Street. The house is now under Interstate 10. My father was a barber, and he owned a shop close by on Brooklyn Avenue. I was the fourth Nava child. Henry, Lucy, and Lola had come before me. After me came Daniel and Rose Marie. The oldest children were Carlos and Helen, born from my mother's first marriage to Ventura Muñatones. Mother rarely spoke about him and only briefly.

Dad's barbershop was always interesting to visit. I recall becoming old enough for my father to let me sweep hair from under the chairs. There were always friends there, even if they were not getting a haircut or a shave, which cost a nickel back then. It was a gathering place, it seemed to me. Behind curtains my father had a small woodshop where he worked on projects when there were no customers. His pals watched as he made harps, guitars, and other musical instruments. One beautiful chess set he made for my mother was of carved ivory. Other chess sets were made of goat horn, which looks just like ivory. I have one chess set made of inlaid different woods. The only harp we have left belongs to Lucy, because he made these items to sell. Dad's friends called him *maestro*. I wondered about this as a boy because he was not a teacher. I later learned it was common among Mexicans to call an artist or craftsman *maestro* if he was very good at what he did. Dad's manual skills have always been an inspiration to me.

Our country was in a terrible economic depression when my memories began. That's why Dad had friends hanging around the barbershop during the day. They were unemployed. The county of Los Angeles gave out food to hundreds of thousands of hungry people. The food came from the federal government. The government bought the food from farmers who could not sell it and sent it to counties for distribution to prevent starvation. This went on year after year. You got whatever there was available. This meant that on one occasion there were only potatoes and raisins, or maybe lots of beets and oranges. Just about everyone in Boyle Heights was on relief, as this program was called. Dad lost his barbershop. I guess most people started to cut their own hair, and men now shaved at home with safety razors.

Father and Mother had not become American citizens. I guess they always dreamed of going back to Mexico. After many years here, Dad did not buy a home even when he could. To buy a home would have been to give up on their dream of returning to El Salitral, which mother still owned. All the other Mexicans we knew felt the same way.

In time, the American government began a program to get rid of immigrants who were "on relief." The Repatriation Program of the 1930s was designed to deport immigrants of all nationalities. Asians and European groups faced oceans to cross so they were harder to deport and were left alone. Mexicans were very numerous, and we came from the country next door, so we were a major target. Employers started asking about your nationality before offering employment, and American citizens were favored for jobs. This increased the number of people on the relief rolls, and thus, Mexicans were vulnerable to cutbacks in employment.

I did not understand what was going on, but suddenly our home was empty of furniture as Mom and Dad sold off what they could at next-to-nothing prices. My mother was heartbroken to lose her Maytag washer and the tall Victor phonograph, which I was now tall enough to wind up. Only some boxes and suitcases lined the walls of the house on Lord Street. My parents decided to go to Mexico because Los Angeles County had cut us from the relief rolls. We children were American born, but that did not matter; all of us were going to Mexico as a family.

I will always remember that house because we lived there during a great earthquake that leveled much of Long Beach. I think it was 1932 when I was taking a lunch bag to Dad's barbershop. The earth shook so much I could not stand up. I stumbled to the most stable thing I could see. I jumped on top of a fireplug and held on for dear life until I could slip down.

I also remember Lord Street because, just down the hill on an open field, Japanese men came to fly kites that went way off into the horizon. The kites were unlike American ones. They were beautiful and looked like birds or flowers. The Japanese kites must have taken much work to build. We made our own kites as fancy as we could, too, but they were very simple by comparison. What struck me was that older Japanese men would spend an afternoon flying kites, just as we children did.

On our last night, the house was packed with friends and relatives. Rather than be put to bed, we stayed up as everyone sang, danced, and ate food that families brought. Dad was a thoughtful sort of fellow. He had many books and liked to talk quietly with friends about politics and philosophy. He was a convinced atheist, which was out of the ordinary in a barrio. While he talked with friends, Mother danced away the evening, for she was the heart of every party. I remember fat Arnulfo dancing with Mother. He had a receding hairline and pasted long hairs forward with some sticky stuff to hide the expanding forehead. Our families were good friends.

A huge box of Baby Ruth candies was among the food. We children pulled down the box from the kitchen counter and hid under the house. Since the house was on a sloping hill, we could stand up underneath where the water pipes and sewer lines ran. Above us the floor shook with dancing and loud Mexican music. I got stuffed with Baby Ruths to the point I could not eat any more. What happened next I learned from others. I got sick to my stomach. Within a couple of hours at dawn, we would board the train just across the Los Angeles River in the beautiful new railroad station built by WPA (Works Project Administration) workers like Dad. The next stop was to be Phoenix, about eight hours away. Luckily, Dad was a health enthusiast and read a lot about medicine. He diagnosed from my fever and pain in the groin that I might have serious internal problems. In a few minutes, I was off to the huge Los Angeles County General Hospital just across the river. Within moments of arriving, I was on an operating table, where they removed my appendix in a rush, judging from the large scar. Rather than going home in a couple of weeks, I was there longer, as tubes drained out liquids from my abdomen. I guess the appendix had burst. The family missed the train and returned from the hospital to pick up the pieces of a demolished life.

It must have been terrible for the family as I lay in the hospital. We had almost nothing left, no furniture, no utensils, and only a few clothes. Some neighbors would not sell back the things we had sold to them very cheaply. Dad had no barbershop and no job. It was years before Mother got another washing machine. I remember doing my part washing my own clothes on a washboard in a bucket of water.

Branches of the family helped us with food and supplies. Lucy's godmother was especially helpful. Her husband had a steady job as a foreman at the huge brickyard in Maravilla, as Mexicans called it. This countryside area in East Los Angeles was called "Miracle" by Mexicans because a community had sprung up like a miracle to house the Mexican immigrant workers of the brickyard.

Other members of the extended family helped us find a place to live close to Bridge Street Elementary School, where I remember kindergarten nap sessions. I did not graduate there because we moved out of the barrio way across town. I remember all my teachers at Bridge Street as wonderful persons. Mrs. Ache was something special. Her voice boomed out like a foghorn. She was very tall, large, and like a four-wheel-drive truck. She was the only teacher ever to spank me. She caught me speaking Spanish one day, and had me come to the head of the class. There she launched me across the floor with one blow to my fanny. As I sailed forward, she boomed out, "Speak English, Julian. You are an American."

On Fridays she would sing for us if the class did well that week. One day she sang Finnish folk songs as she played the piano. After one of these, she turned around and her eyes were wet. She insisted that we learn "Finlandia," which it turns out is the Finnish national anthem. I can still hum my way through "Finlandia." I fancied going there someday because it was Mrs. Ache's homeland. I loved Mrs. Ache, no matter what. Sixty years later, I drove through Finland and recalled much about Mrs. Ache, my lovable frau.

Mrs. Strong had a much better voice, however, and she was a sweetheart of a person. She loved folk music. I can still picture her turning the piano around so she could lead us in singing:

Put on da skillet
Put on da lead
Mammie's going to bake a little shortnin' bread,
That ain't all she's going to do,
Mammie's going to make a little coffee, too (so forth).

Mrs. Strong would bellow out "Allá en el rancho grande" with us. Spanish was okay with her because she said it was a beautiful language.

On my last day at Bridge Street School, I remember that Mrs. Benton gave me a big hug and said, "Always do the very best you can, Julian," as she slipped a quarter into my pocket. Twenty-five cents was a lot of money for a little kid then.

My brother Henry's godparents were the wealthy members of the extended family. Mr. Reveles was a famous painter. Several of the major movie houses in downtown Los Angeles were decorated with his work. The huge curtains that went up and down to start the shows had enormous paintings he did. It's a shame none of these were ever photographed. The Reveles family lived in a huge house on the west side of town, where only Americans lived. His younger and charming wife was driven by a chauffeur in a large black car. I can still recall her voice, which was like music.

All of a sudden, we found ourselves living in a large, two-story house with a cellar and an attic. I was too young to realize that we could not afford the rent for such a house. The Reveles had made arrangements with a local private school to let us live there practically free. The school wanted to buy the entire block in order to expand. The school figured that neighbors would sell their homes when a bunch of Mexicans moved in. Dad refused to let the boys shine shoes to earn pocket money, but he did let my brother Daniel and me operate a newspaper delivery route. During the football season we let cars park on the front lawn for twenty-five cents apiece.

The school's clever scheme failed. We got along fine with the neighbors, and so a year went by and no neighbor sold. After the school cut off our lease, we moved to a small house farther south on 66th Street. Years later, the Harbor Freeway wiped out the entire block the private school had wanted. I smile in revenge at national schools alongside the Interstate 10 and Figueroa Street every time I drive south from downtown L.A. Their plan to use prejudice for business purposes had failed.

Living among Americans was an interesting experience. We were the only Mexicans in the neighborhood. Daniel and I made good friends and even formed a gang that walked down nearby alleys to steal fruit from trees that hung over some fences. We had mixed feelings about this, but we did it for food. We made up drawings of alleys and the state of the fruit and conditions in order to go to the right places where getting caught was less likely. Nothing bad ever happened.

The barrio called us back when I was entering junior high school. I felt at home back in East Los Angeles, but then I had been happy living among Americans also. They were no different than the numerous nationalities I had grown up with. Looking back, all of the Nava children never developed prejudices in view of our integrated childhood experiences and the outlook of our parents.

Hollenbeck Junior High School was brand new. We lived on the very limit of the attendance zone, and so it was a long walk to school every day. Several friends walked to school together, and to break up the monotony, we often found a new route. In time this made me aware of just about every street in that part of town. Hollenbeck had several new features, like loudspeaker communication between the principal's office and each room. It was in this manner that we heard President Roosevelt's address to Congress after the attack on Pearl Harbor. I was in a drafting class and could not really understand what was happening. Our teacher spoke to us very somberly after the president's speech and urged us to study even harder because we might have to help defend our country before long. I enjoyed drafting class because it taught me about things in space and how to put them down on paper.

I loved wood shop classes also. In fact, we still have some furniture pieces I made in wood shop. Both drafting and wood shop opened up my mind to imagining, drawing plans, and making something new. I didn't realize it then, but Mexican boys like me were simply scheduled into shop courses instead of more academic classes. It was a form of discrimination, granted, but it turned out to be a blessing because I have used those abilities in many ways later.

One of my favorite teachers was Dave Schwartz, our gym coach. He was rugged, tall, and handsome. He kidded the Mexicans a lot, and we kidded him back because he was Jewish. I'll never forget the swat Schwartz gave me with a paddle when I was caught in the hallway without a pass. The rules were firm because the boys were becoming young men and the girls were developing attractive figures. I guess the hormones required all the control teachers could muster. I went to the vice principal's office, dropped my trousers, bent over and grabbed my ankles. A terrible swat stung my butt. No self-respecting guy would cry out, so I held my breath as the trousers came up and then walked out stiffly. In spite of the pain, I was now "one of the guys."

After that, I did not see Dave Schwartz again for twenty-five years. By now I was elected to the Los Angeles Board of Education. Board members were debating whether corporal punishment should be abolished. The public was sharply divided, and, due to the controversy, television cameras and people crowded the auditorium. The school principals' association favored continuation of the practice with some modifications. These included having a witness for the paddling and discontinuation of the use of paddles perforated with holes to make them move faster. Dave Schwartz was now retired and served as an officer of the principals' association. He presented a good case for paddling, but the board made history by ending corporal punishment that evening.

Schwartz certainly knew me by name, but I could tell that he was not sure I recalled him as our eyes met during his presentation. After the meeting, TV newsmen took statements from board members and notable citizens for the news. I walked over to Schwartz and greeted him warmly:

"Good to see you again, coach."

"How do you do, Dr. Nava? You do remember me?"

"I sure do."

"Any hard feelings?"

"No. I had it coming, and I paid my dues."

"Did that affect your vote to end swatting?"

"Not at all. I voted on principle."

"I see. No hard feeling on my part, either."

Folks nearby could only wonder why we burst out laughing.

The Second World War had begun in 1939 when Germany invaded Poland, but because I was twelve years of age, war was not real to me. Movies gave me an idea, but the war seemed to have little to do with us. But, of course, it did. All of the school shop classes were building small, black-painted models of Japanese warplanes to very precise detail. These were used for civil patrol observers and the armed forces as well. Everyone talked about a possible attack on the West Coast. People got fined if any light slipped by their window shades after dark. From Boyle Heights you could look down on Los Angeles, and at night some of us would walk to the cliff overlooking the Los Angeles River and marvel at a city below us in total darkness.

On Monday, December 8, by pure chance my cousin Art Nava was the very first to enlist in the navy recruitment center in the new Federal Building on Main Street. He had gotten up before dawn and was the first in a very long line of young men. My brother Henry would soon walk up those stairs and join the navy, too. My turn to walk up those stairs would come as soon as I was seventeen. It was weeks before we heard from our cousin Julian, who was a marine in the middle of the attack at Pearl Harbor. Julián Escobedo was a direct descendant of General Escobedo, a hero at the Battle for Puebla on May 5, 1865. Julian was a career marine, and we all admired his huge chest.

By now I was aware of how poor we were. My oldest brother Carlos had married, and so there were fewer men to help care for the family. Dad was worn out from manual work in the WPA program, building roads, bridges, libraries, and sewer lines. Like many thousands of others, Dad dug ditches for little pay. His hands that could make harps were now rough and stiff. Finally, he found employment as a barber again. He was a broken man now and drank more than he should from the wine that our Italian neighbors made in their backyard.

During the long walk home one evening, a car ran him down. In the huge county hospital near our home, he died a few days later from lack of proper care. The injuries themselves would not have been fatal. This was the same hospital that had saved my life a few years earlier. It never fails that as I drive by on the freeway, I look at the spreading complex of hospital buildings and think, "Okay, one life for another; we are even."

I am sure Dad would have objected to his funeral in the church we attended. Mother had left the Catholic church of her youth and we now attended a Spanish-speaking Presbyterian congregation. I think Mother preferred a Pentecostal church nearby because it was more emotional. We called these worshipers "Holy Rollers" because some yelled out, rolled in the aisles, and punctuated sermons with loud amens. In contrast, the Presbyterian church was dignified and well organized.

How we changed churches is worth telling. The Spanish-born priest at St. Anthony's Church nearby argued that this world did not really matter compared to eternal life so we should not complain to God about our poverty. After some time, he got a stern lecture from Mother about the need for church charity here and now. Both Pentecostal and Presbyterian churches shared clothes and food among the congregation. When he sternly scolded her for endangering the souls of her children by visiting a Protestant church, she told him that was the last he would see of the Navas. We lost many Catholic friends due to Mother's revolt, but we gained new ones who were better for us. This episode burned an anti-Catholic prejudice into me that would affect important life decisions later.

Chapter 3

Our Presbyterian Church Life

Our family life changed greatly, thanks to our becoming members of the Divine Savior Presbyterian Church. In retrospect, the minister and his wife were very far ahead of their time in the barrio. How they related the church to everyday life still surprises me. Their effect on the community is a story in itself. Reverend Hubert Falcón and his wife, Guadalupe Negrete, were a major influence on our lives. Our Spanish improved because all sermons and activities in church were in correct Spanish, not barrio slang. For numerous celebrations, Easter, and Christmas, we enjoyed plays in the church's small theater, where the church members staged rather elaborate shows. All this made a big impression on us children, which I guess was the idea. The young people had various groups dedicated to their needs according to their age groups. "Christian Endeavor" was the group for teenagers. It had elected officers, meetings with formal agendas, and activities, such as trips to the mountains and beaches. In summer, many youngsters would go to Camp Juárez in the San Gabriel Mountains. Numerous romances emerged during such outings, but they were always most proper. I will never forget the two times I went to Camp Juárez with my gang of church friends. We met young people our ages from other Spanish-speaking Presbyterian churches in greater Los Angeles. At annual conventions, church choirs competed for recognition. These and other activities were directed by the Falcóns, who had the genius to involve volunteers from the barrio and wealthy American donors.

As the war went on, more and more young men from our church went into military service, most before they were drafted. We always honored them in church services, including mourning the deaths of some. Church life was an extension of Mexico, but there was no doubt we were all Americans. When the WACS (Women's Auxiliary Corps) was formed, some of our girls joined that outfit also. When one of my circle, Beatrice, returned from boot camp, she was simply beautiful in her uniform and now had a man's handshake.

One of the products of the Depression and prejudice was the emergence of Mexican gangs, called "pachucos," made up of poor boys who had become alienated from both Mexican and American identities. These boys wore long, greasy hair pulled back like a duck's rear end. They wore baggy trousers that were closed tight at the ankles, and they often used broad-rimmed black hats, as well as long key chains at their sides. Most pachucos were otherwise typical teenagers. When they engaged in violence, it was directed at each other over the rights to turf. Anyone entering the barrio from foreign territory ran the risk of getting beat up, which only provoked revenge. Gang wars sometimes caused stabbings and deaths. The urban newspapers called them scum and encouraged the police to deal harshly with them. Frankly, the police often beat up on the young pachucos and jailed them for no cause except for how they looked. All this only made pachucos stick closer together.

Like a fever, pachucos sprang up in barrios all over the Southwest. The pachucos were not really a menace to society, and most could have been turned around with understanding, but they caused fear among everyone in the barrio. Some girls joined gangs also and were shared sexually among gang members to develop a feeling of family. What these young people truly needed was a feeling of acceptance, belonging, and hope in their lives. Many immigrant parents were dysfunctional when it came to adapting to American life and helping their children fit into mainstream society. Mexican barrios were a part of Mexico in the United States. In families with such conditions, many young people sought guidelines for conduct somewhere else. Hostile portrayals of them in radio, movies, and newspapers only made matters worse. Within the infamous Hollenbeck Jail of East Los Angeles, some pachucos had fatal accidents, which were papered over.

Our parents and church encouraged us simply to stay away from pachucos, or "zootsuiters," as they were also called by outsiders. Fortunately, our church life was all-inclusive, so there was no temptation to associate with them. The fact that I never saw a Protestant dressed like a zootsuiter was evidence of successful education linked to religion. Just the same, when their turn came to serve their country in uniform, pachucos were as brave as any others in the U.S. forces. In fact, Mexican Americans in general became outstanding servicemen, as their military decorations proved.

For the Nava children, church life included everything we needed to grow up. My love for fine music probably started with singing in the choir. I had a crush on pretty Conchita, who played the organ. She returned the sentiments, but her parents had loftier ambitions for her, and I resented them for that. She was my first romance, and it never got as far as a kiss. She would have been a blind alley overall. In spite of the music, her world had a rather small diameter.

I have many fond memories of my childhood, even if looking back, I later realize that we suffered prejudice for being Mexicans. During the summer, we joined other Mexicans from our barrio and went to the Simi Valley to pick apricots. Farmworkers were needed in large numbers because the fruit had to be picked quickly as it ripened and there were labor shortages due to the war. We lived in tents supplied by the grower. During the day, the tents were laid out in rows under the huge trees on a carpet of sand. Men shook the trees, and the children and women picked the fruit and were paid by the number of buckets. Daniel and I played at it to see who could fill more buckets. At suppertime, mother cooked on a wood fire. Later, families gathered around to talk and sing to guitars under the stars. I guess we were being exploited, but I will never forget those summers. On weekends, the children walked into Moorpark, about five miles down the dark highway. At the movie house, Mexican farmworkers were ushered to sit on either side of the theater, while Americans sat in the middle.

Back In the city, we knew which movie theaters did not welcome us, and so we avoided them to dodge the embarrassment. Ironically, in downtown Los Angeles, the beautiful movie houses on Broadway and Hill Street, where we were not welcome, now show only Spanish-language movies. Oddly enough, the Americans living on the fringes of the barrio died off in time, and their children moved away to greener pastures. Today, Mexican Americans and refugees from Central America have come to supply all the population in those areas, which have become like a little Mexico. At the Montebello public swimming pool, we were welcomed only on certain days, which were not posted, but we knew because the word got around. We never protested against such conduct, but rather accepted it as the way things were. Our parents used to avoid going where we were not welcomed because it was bad manners to impose our presence or below our dignity to protest. The barrio of East L.A. was our safe haven among other Mexicans, Jews, Japanese, and other minority groups, who all got along fine.

Chapter 4

Aviation Machinist Mate Third Class

World War II caught up with our family. My brother Henry married Vera just before he went overseas, and so he did not see his daughter, Irene, until war's end. Just after boot camp, he came home on leave and accompanied me to see a school counselor at Roosevelt High School. Henry wanted me to take science and math courses so that I could avoid dangerous military duty in the near future. The counselor resisted transferring me from an auto shop major to an academic major because of my low grade point average. At this point Henry stood up in his tight-fitting blue uniform and sternly announced that his younger brother would catch up on his academic deficiencies and take college prep courses. When Henry gave me a stern look, I agreed. The counselor felt threatened when Henry leaned over the desk to deliver his demands and gave in. Almost out of revenge, he scheduled me for physics, algebra, and geometry for the next semester, with the second course of each subject for the following semester, plus solid geometry. Although all this was new and difficult, I got passing grades. Physics and geometry were rational and therefore easier to figure out. Algebra was a problem and is still largely mysterious to me. My classmates were now Japanese and Jewish for the most part, with only a few Mexicans like me.

The Japanese neighborhoods were now all occupied by

Mexicans because of the Japanese relocation. Right after Pearl Harbor, all Japanese people were rounded up and shipped to detention camps in the isolated Owens Valley desert. All our Japanese classmates were gone before we could say good-bye. No one in the barrio blamed them for the attack on Pearl Harbor, but our government questioned their loyalty. I will never forget the truckloads of people leaving like cattle. The lucky ones went in buses. They had to leave their furnished homes behind, for most could not find buyers on such short notice.

We would curse the "Japs" in Japan, but not our neighbors, whom we knew as respectful citizens and hard workers. War movies pictured "Japs" as cruel and heartless. Horrible battles were taking place in the Pacific, and the stories of survivors added weight to the hatred for Japan, which the media promoted. Oddly enough, Germany was not the object of so much hatred. Communist Russians were our "brothers," so our differences with the communists were set aside as schools, movies, and official news reported the brave struggle of the Russians against Hitler. In school we learned the names of Russian commanders, such as General Timoschenko and General Zukov.

More and more members of our church were entering the military. Although the war in Europe was drawing to a close, everyone dreaded the Pacific war so far away and against the Japanese, an enemy who preferred death to surrender. Rather than be drafted into the army, I volunteered for the navy air corps. Thanks to the academic courses I had rushed to take, I was accepted as a potential pilot. My brother Daniel and our friends had built model airplanes for several years, and we were intrigued by flying. Since I dreamed of being an airline pilot someday, here was my chance to fly.

Our church gang of about seven saw me off for boot

camp in Tennessee from the new Union Station. They sang *ranchera* songs for me as the train pulled away. A three-day trip took almost five as our train was pulled off on a side track now and then to make way for long speeding trains loaded with planes, tanks, and trucks. What an adventure! Everyone ought to serve some time in the military, if you ask me. Military service, even in peacetime, can make you appreciate life, family, and your country more.

Boot camp was just as terrible as everyone predicted. It was hot and humid in Tennessee, where we were subjected to ruthless physical training and brainwashing. I had never been in a physical fight, as had many teenagers in East Los Angeles, but here I was learning how to kill and cripple quickly.

From there we were shipped to Oklahoma for technical and flight training. I suffered my first great disappointment during the dental examination. I was turned down for pilot school because I had several cavities. The civilian dentist agreed that, when fixed, these would never bother me in flight. However, the navy ruled out anyone for pilot training with more than three cavities, even if the candidate for flight school was a perfect physical specimen. I could still fly, but as a mechanic/gunner. In retrospect, the naval air force used teeth to make social distinctions. Virtually all navy pilots were white and economically advantaged. Their families had avoided cavities in their children.

I grew up personally in the navy and gained the education I could never have gained in civilian East L.A. For the first time, I stopped being a Mexican. Our platoon was a mixture of every group, except blacks. In this war American blacks were segregated into mostly support units, not fighting units. Only one air force group consisted of segregated blacks.

Warren Richardson, who was precisely my height and weight but very blond and handsome, had been raised in West L.A., but he had never seen a Mexican up close. He asked a lot of stupid questions that turned me off at first. He liked to call me Tonto, the name of the Indian sidekick of the western movie hero, the Lone Ranger. I gave up trying to shake the nickname, but figured Rich was okay when he confessed to me one day, "I wish I had your tan."

Rich and I developed a friendship and a ferocious rivalry in everything, such as running, climbing ropes, swimming, wrestling, shooting, and course work. This was the first time I realized that I was truly as good as anyone else. Being a Mexican had nothing to do with how well I did. Performance was up to me.

Graduation from the Naval Air Technical Training Center was upon us, and assignments split up good friends. Some of us went to gunnery and flight training in Florida. I placed second in gunnery, so I was permitted to pick the turret I would fly in within the giant, four-engined PB4y2, the biggest plane in the navy at the time. In the tail turret you saw only the sky slip away from you. Practically touching me, a fifty-caliber machine gun was at each shoulder. Even ear plugs did not muffle their roar. Since these were our lifeline, we had learned to assemble them or troubleshoot them blindfolded. We were so very good at everything we did. When at last we graduated and got our wings, the sky fell.

The United States dropped the atom bomb, and Japan surrendered. We were dumb with disappointment. The war had ended, and all this training would never be put to use. On the night we got the news, the plane crew went into town and got drunk. It was the first and last time I have been drunk. We piled empty beer cans up to the ceiling in a huge pyramid. The bartender thought it was interesting until it fell down in a huge disaster. He chased us out and called the military police after vulgar language was exchanged. We got away because, although drunk, we could vault over taller fences better than the MPs could.

Chapter 5

From the Barrio to College

Upon separation from the navy, I went to work in a shop that made truck bodies. I had worked there as a janitor in the afternoons during high school. The owner was German American and liked Mexican things. Henry came to work there also. Our skills with tools earned us good money until I decided to go to a local community college. The G.I. Bill of Rights offered scholarships for veterans, as well as help in buying a home. I was no longer simply a barrio boy. I was a veteran, proud of it, and anxious to carve out a future beyond the neighborhood where I had grown up.

When I started college, I broke up with my first sweetheart, Yolanda. As a traditional Catholic barrio girl, she wanted to get married right away, for she was nineteen and in danger of spinsterhood. The prospect of waiting four years was terrible for both of us. Yolanda was tall, slender, and as beautiful as her mother had been. There were rumors in the barrio that her mother had been one of Pancho Villa's women until he changed models—which he did regularly. I thought that maybe Yolanda was one of his many children. The chronology didn't quite fit, however.

I broke up with Yolanda for two reasons. I could not get married before entering college, and she was Catholic. Now, such a problem as religion would not be as important as it was then. In the barrio, there was a social fence between Catholics and Protestants. Yolanda married a mutual acquaintance named Roy soon after we broke up. I never liked Roy and the feeling was mutual. At least he learned firsthand that even after several years of dating Yolanda, I had respected her. Roy married a virgin because my religious experience demanded that I respect her. Those were the personal moral values of the time.

Although I am glad about the way things worked out for me, I have never been proud of breaking up with Yolanda because my decision was motivated by selfishness. How can you choose between someone else's happiness and your own in the long run? Some ten years later, I ran into Yolanda at a supermarket in East L.A., and we spoke for a while as if nothing bad had ever happened. She had two children and was even more gorgeous. We kissed good-bye, and she tasted the same. I never saw her again. Why do I count my decision as a failure somehow, even as I look at my wife, children, and grandchildren with such complete pleasure?

I felt at home in college and earned good grades because after the military service, I had a firm understanding of life. I joined the tennis team and made varsity right away. The ski club introduced me to a new sport that was the nearest thing to flying. I was elected student body president at East Los Angeles Junior College. My secretary was Mitzi Itsihara, a Japanese neighborhood friend from before the relocation. While I was in the navy, she had been in a relocation camp. I was ashamed of what my country had done to Japanese Americans. I likened it to the repatriation of Mexican Americans. Both groups had served their country with distinction during the war. No Japanese resident alien had ever been accused of disloyalty. In fact, a Japanese segregated unit fought with great distinction in the European theater. For their part, Mexican Americans had become the most decorated ethnic group during the Second World War, as they were to be in the Korean and Vietnam wars. I think I know why. My sentiments may have been general in that I wanted to prove I was as American as anyone else.

I decided to become a teacher due to the inspiration of one of my professors at "East," as we called East Los Angeles Community College. Helen Miller Bailey taught social sciences with great skill and inspiration. She took a special interest in Mexican Americans, advising us in many things and inviting some to her home in the mountains nearby. Her husband had been my physics teacher at Roosevelt High School, so I was almost one of her family. "Doc," as we called her, was always there to lend you a few dollars for books or to scold you lovingly for not doing well.

Another teacher who taught English encouraged me to apply to Pomona College. She had attended Pomona and told me all about it. Student life was described as "gracious living" for a student body of only one thousand students. It would be better for me, she claimed, than UCLA, which was already so large that you could call it a factory. Although I had only a B-plus average, my teacher guessed that I might still get into Pomona, where all student applicants had straight-A averages. She explained that grades were not everything that Pomona would take into account. My well-rounded background, military service, and election as student body president could help gain acceptance.

I went to Pomona for my last two years of college and earned my bachelor of arts degree. There were approximately four Spanish-surnamed students there and two blacks, as I recall. Among the 1,000 students, about 600 were males and 400 were women. More men postponed marriage for graduate school than did women, so this provided just about one man for every woman. This made for a high rate of marriage among the graduating seniors. Pomona then and now depends on graduates for its support. Married Pomona students tended to be more generous than single graduates. Everything at Pomona was very well thought out.

Gracious living at Pomona College meant being well dressed for classes and formal meals. The enormous Frary Dining Hall was presided over by a huge mural of Prometheus painted by José Clemente Orozco, one of Mexico's greatest artists. Chapel attendance was not required, but expected. During chapel services, I greatly enjoyed the excellent organ music and the choir. Special lectures and concerts were stimulating, and our professors were the very best. Classes were small, and high performance was taken for granted. I had to study extra hours daily and do daily chores; my only relaxation was the varsity tennis team.

One rainy night, a dear friend was killed riding in my car. We were double-dating on our way to a highway hamburger joint called "Stinky Joe's." My date sat alongside me, and Bob Upham sat on the door side of the coupe with his date on his lap. I started out slowly because the car engine was still cold. Another car slammed into our rear and demolished my restored 1929 Chevy coupe. Neither of the girls was hurt at all. I did recall the wreck when I awoke in a hospital some time later. Bob had been knocked out also, but he never woke up. Bob's parents sued everyone in sight, including me. Pomona College hired a bright young former graduate to represent me at no cost in the lawsuit that was to last over a year.

By this time, I had met Sue Sizer at Pomona, and before long we had fallen in love. Sue was a senior when I was a junior. I met her mom and dad when they came out from Michigan for her graduation. During that next Christmas, I went to Michigan to spend the vacation with her family. By then we had decided to marry, but I asked for her hand anyway. For me it was a cultural thing to ask formally for the hand of the girl you sought to marry. The answer was not an issue, but they appreciated the formality. They realized that I was older than most juniors because of time spent in the military, that I had a serious outlook on everything and wanted to get a Ph.D. I was a little overwhelmed by the Sizer family. During the visit I learned that her dad was vice president of Marshall Field and Co., one of the nation's most eminent department stores.

Sue wanted us to marry during Christmas and drive back to Pomona, where I would finish my last year. I had just applied for graduate studies at Harvard, and gaining acceptance was a major question. Another was the lawsuit over Bob's death. I persuaded her to wait until I graduated and the lawsuit was over, so that we would not have these clouds hanging over our heads. She was willing to work while I finished school and take her chances alongside me on the lawsuit. I had a long talk with her dad, and he understood why I preferred to wait in order to come to the marriage with no problems in my hands. Looking back, Sue was hurt more than I realized.

During the last semester at Pomona, Sue and I wrote constantly. Suddenly, one letter was different from the others. She told me that she was going to marry a graduate student in geography at Northwestern University. The next day I flew back to see her, but she was already selecting her silver. Her mom and dad were truly very sorry, but they were now helping her prepare for the big event. I returned to Pomona as a torn-up young man. With final exams coming up, graduate school acceptance pending, and the lawsuit now in court, this was probably the worst time in my life until then. I could hardly sleep or concentrate from the depression, but I survived.

It is still hard to remember this ordeal. Upon reflection, it was pride that moved me to insist upon waiting for graduation to marry, acceptance to graduate school, and resolution of the lawsuit. On other occasions, pride was to hurt me again.

One of the main concerns I had was that I had applied to only one graduate school. Usually students wanting to enter graduate studies apply to three or four in hopes of getting at least one offer. Pomona Professor Hubert Herring was somewhat of an oddball as well as a great teacher and wonderful person. He put it very simply. Graduate schools compare notes on who has applied to them, and so they know you are shopping around. However, if you apply to only one graduate school and explain why, this approach will impress that school. Since Harvard University had the best Latin American specialist in the nation, Professor Herring said that was the only place for me to go. All of my eggs were in this one basket when I wrote in my application that only Harvard met my needs.

Just before graduation from Pomona, I was accepted by Harvard. And, right after graduation from Pomona, the jury found that I was not responsible for Bob's death. How proud my mother was at my graduation. The ceremony took place in the enormous auditorium we called Big Bridges Hall. The great English historian Arnold Toynbee gave the commencement address, and the music for the procession was out of this world. When I tried to tell mother that Harvard would be even more impressive, this beautiful old lady from Tepetongo just looked up with disbelief. She did not even have any idea where Harvard University was.

Chapter 6

A Barrio Boy at Harvard University

During the summer of 1951, I worked in a shop making fire engines—big, red fire engines. Thanks to my high school shop courses and the navy mechanical training, I qualified for the complicated work, which paid very well. I would need every dollar I could earn for graduate school.

You get rather messy doing this work. The owner's son ran the shop and treated me like he treated the other Mexicans in the shop, since I looked no different. He respected our work, but you could hardly expect him to ask me out for lunch. One day he asked if I was going to stay on after summer because the company had just gained a contract for several engines and he had to assure a full crew. He took a step back when I mentioned that I had just graduated from Pomona College and would soon be off to Harvard for Ph.D. studies. He had graduated from Pomona himself, he confessed. He was very surprised that this messy-looking Mexican had also. And as if that wasn't enough, his worker was going to Harvard. I still savor the satisfaction of seeing his surprise.

It was a long train ride from Los Angeles to Cambridge, Massachusetts. In those days the train cost less than an airplane. The fall season in New England was more beautiful than I had imagined. The changing fall colors of the trees overcame me. Before long the trees were bare, however, and the cold snow arrived. The winds off the Atlantic were colder than the mountains of southern California during ski season. I made good use of a long wool coat given to me by Ignacio López, an aging newspaperman. He had lived back east for a while. When he heard about the scholarship for Harvard gained by a certain young Mexican boy, he looked me up and came from a long distance to give me his long wool coat. Frankly, I would have frozen without that coat. He said, "We can't have the first barrio boy at Harvard catching his death of cold." This gesture made an indelible impression on me.

Harvard and Boston were an entirely new world for me. People spoke differently, and the subway system was so handy. For the first time, I met Irish people and learned that most of them hated Harvard as a bastion of everything English. How could English-speaking people feel like an oppressed minority? I wondered. I learned that the last thing a "Harvard boy" should do was date an Irish girl. The risks of getting beaten up by Irish boys was too great. How would the boys recognize you? It was your clothes and speech. This was no great problem for me because I was so short on money that a movie once a month with male classmates was just about all I could afford. I went to only one Harvard/Yale football game and could not believe my eyes. Harvard men dating Ratcliffe College girls were dressed in suits, carried picnic baskets, and sipped champagne from tall stem glasses. They hardly paid attention to the game.

Many of these students had attended private prep schools rather than public high schools. This meant that they were primed for precisely the types of assignments they would have. I sometimes asked myself, what am I doing here? Everyone was so smart and well read. Splitting an infinitive or dangling a preposition in speech was rare for them.

At the end of my first semester, I got two B-pluses and

two A-minuses. The department secretary called me in to talk about this problem. It was expected that students would get only A grades, with maybe an A-minus or two at most. If you were not turning out as the university expected, then you could take a master of arts degree and call it quits. I was thoroughly alarmed and promised to do better, and I did. I prepared a daily schedule for study on specific courses down to fifteen-minute intervals. This allowed for eating, sleeping, and the time it took to walk across the campus, as well as short breaks to hear classical music. Achievement standards were not a problem again.

At bedtime I would pray, "Lord, I can't let down my family. Please help me through just one more day." I recall finishing a semester final exam on the philosophy of history. I put down my pen just before the proctor yelled out, "You will stop writing." I said to myself, this is an A final exam. It was.

My doctoral professor urged me to fill a gap in nineteenth-century Venezuelan social history—namely, the political career of a dictator who did much to modernize Venezuela, as Porfirio Díaz had done in Mexico during the same period. Professor Clarence Haring knew many important people in Venezuela and suggested that he could arrange for me to get a lot of cooperation in Venezuela. It turns out he and Professor Hubert Herring at Pomona had a high regard for each other over many years. This connection might explain how I got accepted to Harvard. I learned the great value of connections, and such a network of contacts would be valuable again.

The John Hay Whitney Foundation gave me a $1,000 fellowship to help cover a year's research in Venezuela. Today, that would be ten times as much. I came close to losing the award during the critical interview. The man presiding over the committee was a tall; handsome black man who had a pronounced Harvard accent. This struck me as out of place. He asked me if upon getting my degree, I would promise to return to help my people. I said no, calmly and added, "Although I would probably do that, I don't think such a promise should be a condition of the award." As I waited in the hall for the decision, I thought I had ruined my chances. In a short time, Robert Weaver came out and gave me the good news with a Harvard accent. He also said, "I liked your attitude, Mr. Nava. Good luck."

The airfares worked out so that I could travel to Caracas through Los Angeles at no extra cost. My family was so glad to see me after my being away two years. Much to my surprise, I got kidded a great deal because I spoke English with a Harvard accent. Thanks to this, I gained more understanding for Weaver. It seemed that ways of speaking are rather sticky. I tried to speak normally as quickly as I could, however.

Chapter 7

Doctoral Research in Venezuela

Caracas was a beautiful colonial city when I arrived there in the fall of 1953. The government was in the hands of a military dictator allied to super-wealthy people and the Catholic church. Large sums of money were pouring into the national treasury because of recent oil discoveries in Lake Maracaibo. Venezuela is a very beautiful country with distinct regions and people. People there looked like Mexicans, but they did not act like them at all.

President Carlos Pérez Jiménez was short, fat, and not very bright. He stumbled reading speeches as if it were the first time he was seeing the text. The powerful people around him were rebuilding the country with oil profits, but making fortunes for themselves in the process. American oil companies and merchants were getting their share of this bounty. The vast majority of people were poor. They embodied a mixture of Indians, blacks, and Europeans. Thousands of Europeans were immigrating to Venezuela and were finding ways to cash in on the oil income. President Eisenhower gave a high U.S. military award to this petty dictator because the United States wanted free access to Venezuelan oil.

Living expenses were higher than I figured, so I lived in a very modest but clean boardinghouse that had been built in about 1800. There were twelve other boarders, and we all ate together. My room was 5x12 feet. A weak lightbulb hanging from the ceiling and a narrow coil spring cot were my home for a year.

Since colonial times, Caracas residential addresses were written as a house number between two street corners. My address was "Truco a Guanábano 117," or "Dirty Trick to Pear 117." Dirty Trick corner connected to four other street corners. The same thing applied to the Pear corner. If you did not know the city, it was confusing to find a location.

My Harvard mentor, Professor Clarence Haring, gave me a letter of introduction to a Venezuelan senator, José Antonio Cova. This fat old fox was a good historian with about ten books to his credit. He was also a very politically conservative fellow who backed the dictatorship and thus had a lot of influence. He set up a desk for me in the corner of his huge office and got permission for me to enter the book stack area of the National Library close by, as if I were an employee. Senator Cova had the highest respect for Professor Haring, and this helped me greatly.

Many people walked in to pay their respects to this powerful man. Although I got a boost from Cova, as everyone called him, my research was slowed down by the way the National Library was set up. Books were placed on shelves according to their size and the color of the binding. It made for a very good-looking library. Since the librarians knew where and on what floor the books were, they resisted newer ways to catalog the enormous holdings that went back to colonial times.

Since I had a strict filing system for my notes, if anything was misplaced, it was not my doing. Because now and then notes were a little out of place, I could tell that someone had been looking through my notes. I never mentioned this to Cova during the year I was there.

I traveled by bus to the corners of Venezuela during the

numerous national and religious holidays. Venezuela is a very patriotic country, where Simón Bolivar, the Liberator, gets the veneration of a saint. All these holidays closed the National Library. I explored Venezuela from the high Andes down to the Orinoco River and to the countless oil wells pumping up black gold from Lake Maracaibo.

At one social affair to which my American girlfriend Bobbi Burns invited me, I got acquainted with the local Sears Roebuck manager. I asked him why Sears sold such outmoded models of appliances at such high prices. He stated that Sears would love to sell the same goods we could buy at home at half of what Sears charged for outmoded models in Venezuela. The Venezuelan government would not let them do what Sears wanted to do because Venezuelan industrialists could not compete with Sears products. This favoritism was found all over Latin America. Under the disguise of helping build up local industry, the policy protected the nation's rich merchants and industrialists by giving them a captive market.

My girlfriend surprised me on one of our trips out of town. "Julian, let's be logical about this, as Harvard men are. We would make a fine couple, so let's get married." I knew that graduates of Smith College, like Bobbi, often married Yale or Harvard men. We enjoyed each other's company a great deal. She was pretty and very Irish; that is, she loved poetry, singing, conversation, and Scotch whiskey. Bobbi could talk for hours on endless topics, but especially clairvoyance.

Bobbi was devoutly Catholic, and this troubled me. She was very direct in saying that her husband would be the first man who made love to her. We went by the rules, and so we traveled on overnight trips to many places. Bobbi saw me off at the airport in La Guaira when my work was done. We kept company upon her return to New York City and celebrated my doctorate a year later. Bobbi was a virgin when she married a nice Catholic fellow back in the United States a couple of years later. We wrote to each other for several years at Christmastime, and then the letters dropped off.

On the way back to Harvard, I flew through Panama and stopped off in Central American capitals. The plane landed in Guatemala right after an army officer hired by the CIA overthrew the elected president. The United States claimed he was communist oriented. He was not, as it turned out. He simply wanted land reform and other measures to help the poor. The overthrown president would have reduced American corporate influence in Guatemala; hence, the CIA funded the revolt. I left as soon as I could because soldiers backing Castillo Armas, the new president, were everywhere, with guns at the ready.

I flew out of Guatemala City for Mexico with great relief and stopped off in Tepetongo to see many relatives for the first time. What a charming little colonial town in a mountain valley greeted me. It looked just as Mother had described it. As I drove into town in a taxi, I was startled to see myself walking toward me on the cobblestone streets. The fellow and I stared at each other. I stopped the car to speak to myself. We were cousins. It was Jesús María Flores, son of my uncle Jesús.

After meeting all the relatives, I headed home right away. I was very sick from an infection in my right leg. The trouble started in Venezuela, but it had gotten worse by the time I got to Tepetongo. In view of costs, I took the train to El Paso and then flew to Los Angeles when the fever became uncomfortable. The doctor said I got back just in time because the tropical infection would soon have spread widely. For a year malnutrition had weakened me. With the best drugs, I fought off the strange infection before long. Actually, in Poland forty years later, I developed the very same symptoms in the very same place in my right leg. Doctors eliminated the bug this time with antibiotics that did not exist in 1954. In the tropics there are diseases that we can hardly cope with even today.

While in Los Angeles, I went to work in a Ford automobile plant that paid very well because I was a metal finisher. I straightened out bumps in cars acquired during assembly. However, I needed more money than I could make at the plant for the last year at Harvard. I borrowed $1,000 from Dr. Francisco Bravo. He was a hero in my eyes because he loaned money to Mexican-American medical students. Thanks to the recommendation of City Councilman Edward R. Roybal, Dr. Bravo made an exception to his practice of supporting only medical students and lent me the money to help me finish my last year at Harvard. He was very conservative in every way. He only lent money because he wanted to see that the borrower would invest in himself. Also, as the loans were repaid, they became part of a perpetual fund.

Dr. Bravo produced many Mexican-American doctors in this manner, most of them graduating from Stanford University Medical School. He loved Stanford because this university had helped him with a scholarship while he was a student in its medical school. When Dr. Bravo died, his will left a lot of money to Stanford to maintain his program.

Many years later while on the Los Angeles School Board, I persuaded the board to name a new high school in his honor. The school was to specialize in premedical studies for students from all over Los Angeles. I had long since paid back his loan, and this was just something special for him. With a school named after him, I figured he would continue to help young Mexican Americans as a role model.

Chapter 8

A Mexican-American Ph.D.

Back in Cambridge, I went to work writing the doctoral dissertation while worrying about monthly living expenses. I considered becoming an assistant for some professor to earn money. However, this would take time away from my writing and add an extra year to my completing the degree. Professor Arthur Schlesinger, Sr., who was a giant in American history, told me when I asked him for advice, "Most of what you will learn will come from working in the field, so get out of here as fast as you can. Do what you have to in order to finish quickly."

I was lucky to earn enough money while working only three hours a week. This seemed like stealing the money. Boston General Hospital placed ads for subjects for medical experiments. I signed on to get the substantial pay. My work involved swallowing a ball about the size of a big olive until it reached my stomach. The ball had wires linked to it, and these were connected to instruments. I kept wanting to vomit as I passed the ball and wires down my throat. Once down, I was sweating from anxiety, which was fine for them. I received some injections that made me more nervous. The wires recorded the rise in acid in the stomach and other things I could not understand. Two hours later, I pulled out the ball and recovered. I would pick up a check for a hundred dollars and take the subway back to Cambridge by suppertime. I never told my classmates what I had been doing, except for Richard White, my roommate

The researchers kept me on for some time because I didn't react as they imagined. What they did not know was that I remained calmer than expected because I closed my eyes and simply prayed while the injections were supposed to make me nervous. The researchers just scratched their heads and booked me for the next week. Income from being a medical guinea pig paid my expenses during the last year in Harvard. To my knowledge, no permanent harm was done, even after they increased the dosage, and my pay.

Bobbi would come up on weekends to stay with me, according to the rules. The Irish landlady, who was a busybody, was tuned in to Bobbi's hopes to catch me at a weak moment. The landlady wondered how I could be Mexican and still not be a Catholic. In spite of our compatibility, we did not marry. It was not the difference in religion, for we were very compatible and knew each other well. In view of this, our characters came to light. Bobbi would blow her stack when she got upset. I had never heard my father or mother yell at each other. I could not accept a wife who would act this way when frustrated or angry. This one trait was probably what held me back.

In 1955, I received my doctorate in history. A commencement at Harvard is something to see. Dr. Conrad Adenaur, chancellor of the new West German Republic, was the commencement speaker. I will never forget the ceremony. Classmates who chose to be graduate assistants admired my flashing crimson robes. They would have to wait a year or more to wear theirs. It was hard to believe that I had completed the doctorate in just four years, close to a record, I think. My only regret was that none of my family could afford to come or send my mother to the event.

The professors at Harvard were so brilliant that in my

mind's eye I can still see myself listening to one or the other. They continue to be an inspiration for my teaching. The special lectures and musical performances I also will never forget. After Sunday chapel, a handful of students would stay to hear the organist play and show his stuff for a while. Harvard was a state of mind. You could not buy it or lose it.

College teaching jobs were very scarce at this time. I didn't know why. I applied to many places, and even with a Harvard degree, I could not find anything worthwhile. I recall one offer I did get. A small college in Nebraska offered a heavy teaching load at a modest salary as long as I coached the varsity tennis team and promised not to drink or fornicate in town. During the interview, wondering what life was like in that remote location, I asked how far away the next town was. The interviewers misunderstood my motives and changed their manner of speaking. I declined the offer because I had survived several years of hard winters in New England and I wanted a warmer climate by this time. I knew that Nebraska winters were worse than those in New England.

Chapter 9

Teaching in Puerto Rico

I signed up to teach in Puerto Rico in the fall of 1955. A charming Puerto Rican graduate classmate, Josefina Cintrón, got me the job. We were good friends and talked only in Spanish when we would share a coffee at the cafeteria. She introduced me to her uncle, dean of humanities at the University of Puerto Rico. He was in Cambridge head-hunting, as it turned out. She arranged for the three of us to have supper without telling me what she had in mind. By dessert we had talked about many things in Spanish. He offered me a job then and there with good conditions. I would teach humanities, in Spanish of course. I thought Dean Quintero did not speak English, but as we clarified the employment conditions, he switched to perfect English and bid us farewell. Josefina just smiled with a sparkle in her big black eyes.

My last semester and summer at Harvard were very enjoyable. I spent a lot of time with classmates and got involved with their work for the fun of it. Henry Stengel was building a model of a large development for Fire Island, just off the coast of New England. Professor Walter Gropius saw me around his class so much he thought I was one of his students. I also spent time with my roommate, Richard White. I barely understood what he was doing. I watched him in a giant acoustical laboratory in which you could fit a small blimp. Dick was a brilliant solid-state physicist studying how one could record data in small crystals. His doctoral research came to be the start of the revolution in transistors that followed a decade later. Little crystals that record data have made computers possible. I have always remembered witnessing the start.

While Dick wound up his research, I worked in the Ford assembly plant in Sommerville, Massachusetts. Thanks to earlier experiences working with metal, I got wonderful pay. Metal finishers are important in a car assembly plant, and once you know this line of work, you don't forget it. As the car bodies are assembled, some get bumped and need immediate straightening out before they can be bathed in acid and painted. There was so much noise along the assembly line that I talked and yelled at the car as I smoothed out the dents. I was actually talking to myself in order to put up with the pressure as the cars rolled down the assembly line endlessly. I earned enough money that summer to buy a used car, rebuild the engine, and put on new tires for the trip home.

Dick White and I drove across the country late that summer. I contributed the car, and Dick paid for the gas from coast to coast. It is sad that such an adventure could not be enjoyed with safety today. We camped out anywhere we liked, cooked, and at night crawled into our sleeping bags. When we got to Los Angeles at last, Dick insisted we keep on going to the end of Wilshire Boulevard until we reached the Pacific Ocean, which he had never seen. As he put it, we had driven from sea to shining sea.

Dick took off for the Bay Area and a job anxiously waiting for him. My visit home was short. All of the family were so proud of me. One of my young nephews asked, "Uncle, how come you talk funny?" My sister Rosemarie replied, "Well, I didn't want to say it, but you have picked up a Harvard accent again, Julian." Fortunately, it washed away during two years in Puerto Rico. In a purely Spanish-speaking world demanding domination of academic terms in Spanish for teaching and discussing, I felt clumsy the few times I had to speak in English.

Puerto Rico was the loveliest place I had ever seen. The tropical island had cool mountain areas where hillbilly people lived. Other Puerto Ricans called them *jíbaros.* Actually, a *jíbaro* was simply anyone who lived in the countryside, was poor, and had little education. City folk tended to look down on them, even though much of what was authentic Puerto Rican culture was of *jíbaro* origin. I had to speed up my Spanish constantly in order to get along. Folks on the island talk twice as fast as Mexicans, and since they do not pronounce final consonants, my ear had to adjust. They made fun of Mexican Spanish for being so slow by comparison. By the time I left, two years later, I was still tagged as a Mexican, even though I thought I had passed as a *borinqueño* (Puerto Rican).

Public schools in Puerto Rico produced students with many academic deficiencies, while private or parochial schools produced students well prepared for college. The differences in learning were mostly a reflection of family wealth and parental support for the students. Generally, poverty produced low reading, writing, and math skills.

I was fascinated to be part of Operation Bootstrap at the university level. Schools of education at Columbia University and the University of Chicago had helped the University of Puerto Rico develop new college entrance examinations for high school graduates. These tests measured basic aptitude and capacity for university level studies. They avoided achievement exams, which are commonly used in the United States to determine college entrance. Since *jíbaros* comprised 90 percent of Puerto Rican high school graduates, entering freshmen were often deficient in specific knowledge. However, the college entrance tests were accurate in measuring basic intelligence and capability. As long as the student was motivated, experts predicted he or she would succeed in his or her studies.

All the professors were expected to help students overcome their deficiencies, but something else about this educational system was even more important. Freshman and sophomore courses were very carefully designed to cover basic material in a manner that was understandable to an intelligent person with less formal knowledge.

Every Friday, the professors offering a given course met for a couple of hours. Each professor reported on how well students were grasping the essential material and ideas. At these meetings, we shaped the plan of action for the next week. I resisted this guidance of my class work at first. After all, my educational experience in Pomona College and Harvard was totally different. Each professor there was free to do as he thought, and students were accustomed to this form of academic freedom. I saw that the Puerto Rican approach helped students catch up and do just fine by the time they graduated. Independent surveys of Puerto Ricans years after graduation revealed they did as well as American graduates from public universities.

In a sense, I was learning while I was teaching. This Puerto Rican approach to higher education shaped my own teaching thereafter. Affirmative action in higher education was very familiar to me by the time it was invented in the United States in the 1960s.

I fell in love with Anita, a charming university teacher of biology. But I must confess that I was still anti-Catholic deep down, and I let this prejudice bring me to cancel our plans to marry. I went as far as I could with the course offered by the church for non-Catholics planning to marry a Catholic. I just could not stomach the indoctrination, which included historical information I knew was not accurate. Anita could not change her religion any more than I could, so after much soul-searching, we called it quits.

Unexpectedly, my sister Lola telephoned from Los Angeles to tell me that our mother had terminal cancer and very little time to live. I was on a plane the next day with no time to offer good-byes to friends. As the plane climbed over San Juan, we flew over the baseball field where professors and students would play ball all day Sunday. We would follow that with a meal at the open-air faculty club nearby. Life there was very casual and pleasant.

Very soon the plane was over water, and my mind was on mother and the fear that I would get home too late. All of a sudden, I was living with Lola, Jess, and their children in the San Fernando Valley. Mother was living there also and was very glad to see her wandering son. Lola's family and I cared for Mother now. She had been living with my sister Rose Marie before. Within a family like ours, parents never worried about old age and care. Taking care of parents was as natural as breathing. It was a good thing I came back immediately, rather than wait for the end of the semester. I would have missed seeing my mother alive.

Although she was much thinner and pale, Mother was as chipper and pleasant as usual. She rolled herself around the house in a wheelchair and moved her feet to the rhythm of Mexican music. We got her to record a conversation about her childhood in Tepetongo and sat fascinated to hear stories she had not told us before. None of us has ever wanted to play that recording, however.

Mother was attended by Dr. Francisco Bravo, who had lent me money for studies at Harvard. As usual, he was kind but plain-speaking. He said it was wasteful and futile to help Mother more because, if he prolonged her life, she would soon be in great pain before she passed away. Nature should be allowed to take its course. We accepted his opinion.

At the hospital, Mother asked to speak to each of us individually, so the eight children took turns with short intervals, as Dr. Bravo suggested. Mom was all made up and looking very pretty. She looked at my shirt and said blue was my best color. Since Anita had come to Los Angeles after me to visit, hoping for the best, Mother met her and liked her very much. Mom said, however, it was probably better that we not marry because Anita was as sincere in her own faith as I was in mine. Such differences would cause problems later. As my turn ended, Mother said, "Julian, I am soon going to be with the Lord, so I am not afraid, and you should not be either." I kissed her on the cheek and left as the next took his turn to say good-bye. She left us during that night. She helped me to lessen my fear of death.

Mother is buried on a lovely hillside plot in Forest Lawn Cemetery with a long view to the south. She picked this site a long time before, preferring it to a burial site next to Dad in East Los Angeles. She always had a mind of her own. My dad was a dedicated and well-informed atheist. He never accompanied us to church, where we spent all day Sunday with various activities. When he died, she had a full-blown church service for him, even though he was an atheist. The sanctuary was packed. I chuckle about this family scandal as I drive on the Golden State Freeway and look north toward that green hill where Mother lies. The young pine trees planted near her burial site are huge now. Mother's death brought my teaching in Puerto Rico to a sudden end and opened a new chapter in my life.

Chapter 10

Coming to Teach in Northridge

I was contacted by the newly formed branch of Los Angeles State College in Northridge while teaching in Puerto Rico. I was back to see Mother before any decision could be reached on the job offer. I was hired right away and never returned to San Juan. I have been teaching here forty-four years as of the turn of the century.

The new college was located in a pumpkin field and orange orchard. Classes met in World War II dormitories redone into classrooms. The founding faculty became a family because we were small in number and had to work closely to organize everything. While serving in one of many committees, I suggested the matador as our college symbol. The student government agreed with this Hispanic symbol and sent me to Mexico City to bring back some authentic torero outfits and other stuff. I still have my first semester grade books. Looking down from my office now at a campus of more than 25,000 students, these first semester grade books seem like a remnant of another life.

I was still single and free to come and go as I pleased. I lived with Lola until I bought a house in Northridge, making use of my veteran's G.I. Bill of Rights. This federal program made it very easy for veterans to buy a home with no down payment and low interest on the mortgage. The house was big for just me, but I planned to fill it up over time. These early years at the college were very special because in addition to classes, which I enjoyed, I played with the college tennis team and was faculty sponsor of the ski club. That meant I had many friends, and thanks to our climate, enjoyed weekend ski trips in winter to the mountains and to the beach a few days later. Class preparation took much time because teaching was in English now and the courses were on the American model. The students were very well prepared for college work, and so I tried to give them the quality of teaching I had enjoyed in Pomona and Harvard.

Just now a former student walked into my office to say hello. I feel good that he is a college teacher also. In a way, I have been reproducing myself and paying back the help others gave to me along the road to college teaching.

Chapter 11

Pat and I Start Our Married Life in Spain

A search for a wife was always on my mind because I was now thirty-five years old. A former U.S. marine captain, an excellent professor of English, boomed out over coffee, "Julian, it's quite simple. Marry an elementary school teacher or marry money!" It was an order, as Mitch Marcus put it. I sometimes wondered what his classes were like. His classes must have been very structured and good, for he was very popular on campus.

I was having lunch with Ernie Velardi one day. Ernie was a painter of the modernist school whose art work I could not appreciate. I like representational painting, something that looks like what it is. As we talked to each other simultaneously, like good Latinos, two female students walked by whom I had never seen before. One caught my eye instantly. I jumped up from the table, ran over, and said hello to her. She agreed to go for a walk that evening. Ernie thought I was rather impetuous. I replied, "That's odd coming from an Italian who starts a painting without knowing how it's going to turn out."

During the walk around the campus that evening, Pat Lucas told me she had only a year left to graduate and intended to be a kindergarten teacher. Her college dorm was across the street from the newly built Prairie Street Elementary School. We began to take evening walks around the school. How could we guess that our three children would attend that school some time later.

Our relationship had some ups and downs. A few months later, we went separate ways as Pat returned to dating a previous boyfriend and I resumed dating two Barbaras, a Linda, and a Sharon. I won't mention last names to "protect the innocent." Each was a wonderful person, but Pat was always on my mind. Pat agreed to date again some time later. She had moved back with her folks in the west side of the city. This gave me a chance to meet her parents and younger brother, Larry. I liked her parents and their solid family ties. By now we had known each other more than a year.

When Pat agreed to marry me, I went through the traditional ceremony of asking her father for her hand. Of course, he had been tipped off why I was coming over that evening. We married on June 30, 1962, on the mountaintop Presbyterian Church overlooking the San Fernando Valley. Our honeymoon was a long drive along the beautiful eastern slope of the Sierras to Lake Tahoe, over the top and then down the Pacific Coast Highway. This is the most beautiful drive in the country, we think. We traveled this long loop in my 1954 Chevy. Many old Chevys are still on the road. Mexican immigrants bring them back to life from junkyards because they are so reliable, especially with the 350 V8 engine. You can raise the hood and not only understand what's in there, but fix it yourself. We were sadly forced to sell my blue Chevy, and Pat's little antique MG to raise funds for a new adventure.

Within a month of returning from our honeymoon, we were packing for a flight to Spain. I had gained a Fulbright Award to teach in Valladolid, Spain. This provincial city, about 100 miles north of Madrid, used to be the capital of Spain, and folks there still look down on Madrid, which never amounted to much until about 1600.

Poor Pat, she was limited to one suitcase for a year. Before jet planes, luggage weight was a problem. Our weight allowance on the airplane was made up of reference books to teach U.S. history. The Lockheed Constellation carried us across the Atlantic with a lot more vibration and noise than jets make today. Since Pat saves everything, she still has that white, battered suitcase.

We were going to go to Katmandu, Nepal, at first. At the last minute, the opening in Spain popped up. I snatched it because life high in the Himalayan Mountains would have been too much of a cultural change for Pat. Can you imagine Pat's situation? Just married at twenty-three years of age, one suitcase of clothes for a year, going to Europe for the first time, and not speaking Spanish in a provincial city where hardly anyone spoke English. Spain was a major challenge for her; Nepal would have been a little too much. I never gave up the hope of getting to the roof of the world, however. Many years later I did go to the roof of the world in Tibet.

Spain was a very special place in 1962, and so was the region called "Old Castille." This is the land of Queen Isabel and the Christian warriors who led in the centuries-long effort to expel the Moors from Spain. Castillians have never forgotten their past glories, but when we arrived, the people were struggling to recover from a disastrous civil war. Catholic and political conservatives supported by the military were victorious over secular and republican groups. Many European countries took sides and supplied arms to their favorite side. Russia was the main supporter of the republicans, many of whom were socialists, while Germany under Adolf Hitler and Italy under Benito Mussolini supported the Spanish fascist rebels trying to replace the republican government in Spain. Feelings about politics were still very intense because everyone had lost relatives in the heartless fighting of the Spanish Civil War. Republican sympathizers were afraid to speak out and fascists reigned supreme in all walks of life. Presiding over the Movement, as the ruling party was called, was general and dictator Francisco Franco. The population was so tired of war and its destruction that politics just evaporated from social life, it seemed. "El Caudillo," as Franco was called, made all the national decisions, and the parliament obeyed.

To force national unity, Franco ordered the end of public use of any language other than Spanish. This policy was curious to me since Franco himself was a Gallego, an ethnic group from northwestern Spain that enjoyed a distinct language and culture. The Catalans around Barcelona and the Basques on the Pyrenees Mountains were two other groups that posed a problem to cultural national unity. Their languages and the culture were suppressed by law in hope that they would die out in time. Patriots in these regions ran the risk of harassment, imprisonment, or execution if they were caught using a language other than Spanish. All of this was fascinating to a Mexican American whose birthplace was formerly part of his mother's homeland: Mexico.

Anywhere you might be driving or walking at any hour, police might come out of hiding and stop you to ask some questions. The Guardia Civil had very distinctive black uniforms. Their job was to guarantee law and order. These police who always worked in pairs had absolute power, even though they were in practice very polite. They were helpful in the event you had a problem with your car or were lost and so forth. Our personal experience with them was very good. Curiously, you felt completely safe anytime and anywhere. As long as you behaved, you were fine. If you were a troublemaker, you would have much to regret. Under normal circumstances, the two Guardia Civil police bade you farewell with "*Vaya con Dios.*"

Bearing all this in mind, one might wonder why the government in Spain accepted a handful of American professors to offer courses on American history, political institutions, and society. I guessed that by 1962 the old *caudillo* saw his time running out. Perhaps it was time for Spain's university youth to learn about the world and be prepared to function under new conditions. The Spanish Civil War had ended in 1939; this was one generation after that terrible conflict. The State Department coordinated the program for American professors in Spain and told us in a briefing that we were part of a pilot program. It was in our national interest that we succeed and that the cultural and educational exchanges be expanded in order to have influence with Spain's future leaders.

After the briefings from the American embassy in Madrid, we took an old train to Valladolid. The rails must have been repaired many times, and it seemed that the train was in danger of jumping the tracks. We arrived in Valladolid before we were expected and checked into a very old hotel until we could find permanent housing. It was past suppertime, so we walked around town until we dropped into a colorful restaurant. We could not figure out the menu because all the dishes were unknown to us. Aside from the fine wine and bread, I took a chance and ordered *calamares en su tinta*. This thick black soup tasted like nothing else we knew, but it was good. It turned out to be sliced portions of squid cooked in its ink.

After a few days, I found the dean at the university. Although the school year formally started on the first of September, he said we were free until early October. When I asked how I would know when to start classes, he said, "When the students arrive." I thanked the dean, but inside my head I marveled that this university system had lasted so many centuries.

During the free time, we took a train to Belgium to pick up a new VW bug we had ordered from Los Angeles. Rather than pay for shipping the car by train to Spain, we could drive it back and save money. Purely by chance, we were at the factory on the right day and saw our green VW bug roll off the assembly line. A worker jumped in and started the engine for the first time, and we drove off into the city. Upon turning on the radio, we first heard a Dodger baseball game broadcast over the Armed Services Radio Network.

Within a few days, we were in East Berlin, where you could breathe the oppression in the air. Crossing through East Germany into West Berlin, we and the car were thoroughly inspected by communist guards who warned us to not stop on the highway. Tall watchtowers were placed along the *autobahn* within sight of each other. From West Berlin, we went through the famous Checkpoint Charley into the communist part of the city. We stayed there only an hour or so because it was so depressing. Everyone looked down as he walked, and no one talked. Pat and I both remarked how good it was to be an American as we sipped tea and looked at buildings splattered with holes from different sizes of weapons. Thirty years later, I was in those very same places. The bullet marks were still evident everywhere, but by then East Berlin was in the process of rejoining the rest of the city in a united democratic Germany.

Teaching in the University of Valladolid was a unique experience because the university was still so old-fashioned. As in the Middle Ages, an old usher with a long official staff would look into the lecture hall before I could enter. After a ceremonial pause, he would tap the floor loudly with the tall fancy pole, his symbol of authority. I'd walk up to the ancient podium as three hundred students stood at attention. After I said "*buenas tardes,*" they all responded with amazing unity and sat down. Toward the end of the lecture, the old man would crack the rear door open and catch my eye to let me know I had five minutes left. Should I go overtime, the students had the right to simply walk out.

Each lecture was carefully prepared. I had to avoid angering the government agents who, I was sure, were among the students. After all, I was talking about the development of our democratic, open society. I think it helped for me to point out our shortcomings and unfinished business. I described our democracy as a process rather than a finished product.

After the lecture, the students and I would go across the square to a bar for *tapas* and wine. *Tapas* are snacks of all sorts that go well with wine, beer, or coffee. Students and professors had socialized in this manner since the Middle Ages. Probably some of the best communication took place during these informal sessions. I would get home for supper with a good appetite and ready to hear about Pat's adventures during the day.

Pat has stories of her own, but the one I like best is about the first time she went to the central market to buy some chicken for supper. Refrigeration was scarce, so housewives went every day to buy fresh meat and vegetables. Pat could hear women say, "*Ahí viene la americana*" (Here comes the American). Much to Pat's surprise, you could only buy a live chicken. After Pat made herself understood with gestures and some Spanish learned on the firing line, the seller grabbed the poor creature, wrung its neck, and proceeded to pluck its feathers. Pat was aghast at this barbaric procedure. After that, we had only red meat for supper. The steer or lamb was already butchered out of sight, and so this did not offend our American sensitivity. The Spanish Pat learned was Castillian Spanish. By the time we left, she was conversing like a native. Years later, when we were living in Colombia and then Mexico, people there remarked on her Castillian accent, which made them think she was from Spain.

On weekends and holidays we jumped into the VW and drove off in any direction that came to mind. In one isolated Castillian town where we stopped to see wine making, I was taught a lesson I have never forgotten. The owner of the winery was flattered with our interest in the process and invited us to his house nearby for wine, cheese, and bread. It turned out he was a retired fascist cavalry officer who had fought in the Civil War. Most people in this region supported Franco with a passion. We tasted several wines, but one, in particular, was simply divine. He explained that certain noble families in the region had the first rights to buy this wine called Diamante. After the sales to nobles, there was some wine for public sale. I observed that he could expand production and export it for a very good profit because of its superb quality. He looked at me with surprise and asked, "What for?" People in Castille regarded you by how you behaved and not by the money you had. Money did not define you and still does not. This lesson stuck with me because I had observed that in most of Latin America this attitude was also common.

During the Christmas season, we went to ski in Innsbruck, Austria. The views of the Alps from the train were make-believe in their beauty. The innkeeper of the charming lodge must have mistaken us for a couple from the American embassy in Spain. To save money, we had bought the cheapest tour package, but due to this misunderstanding, we ended up in a suite with every service you can imagine. Only as our stay was ending did we figure out why we were receiving such treatment, but we didn't have the heart to correct the mistake. I paid for my sins afterward, however.

Coming down a ski slope, I stopped to catch my breath,

and in an instant I saw stars as I was catapulted forward. A speeding skier had slammed into me at full speed. Pat said that he cartwheeled down the slope and kept going as I sprawled out half-conscious. It took me a month before my right shoulder healed. Pat had to drive because I could not shift the transmission.

Winter was endless in Valladolid. Our furnished apartment had very high ceilings for protection against the summer heat. The only heating was a small potbellied stove that burned coal. We huddled around it to read, compare adventures, and make plans for the future. All the furniture really belonged in a museum, which is what we called the place. The rent was next to nothing. The bed was a monstrosity of ancient carved oak. However, we took pictures of it because that is where we conceived our daughters, Carmen and Katie, as we fought off the cold.

Holy Week in Valladolid must be seen to be believed. For a week the city was made dark at night because all the lights were turned off. Everyone in the city gathered for the religious processions that went on late into the night. Religious statues taken out of churches were placed on platforms for the annual parade. Only candles lit the platforms carried through the dark streets on the shoulders of some twenty men. The heavy platforms swayed left and right as the men walked in step along the long route. Thousands stared in complete silence. The wavering candlelight made the statues come to life.

It was an honor to help carry a platform. Christian brotherhoods had done this since the Middle Ages. These brotherhoods, or *hermandades,* as they were called, were made up of members known only to each other. On such occasions the brotherhoods paraded with their distinctive robes, their heads covered by hoods to hide their identities. They looked just like the Ku Klux Klan, or rather, the clan looked like the brotherhoods that antedated them by many centuries.

Since about 800 A.D., these groups formed to fight against the Moors that occupied the peninsula. To avoid persecution, they hid their identities and kept very accurate records of Christian family names. These brotherhoods combined religious faith and patriotism in a very powerful mixture that nourished the seven-hundred-year struggle to expel the Islamic rulers. Brotherhood and church records kept files on the military decorations each family earned, which they painted on their coats of arms. Therefore, Spanish surnames and their coats of arms can be traced back many centuries to where the earliest records begin. The coats of arms, or symbols painted on shields, served as identification during battle. The wood-carved coat of arms for the Nava family, which we have hanging, carries on this tradition. Hispanic youngsters dropping out of school today by the thousands don't know that their family names, whether Sánchez or García, have a valiant, recorded past. Today's struggle is not against some invader, but rather how to realize one's potential in spite of handicaps.

Soon after the discovery of America, the Spanish monarchs prohibited the building of castles and discouraged the use of coats of arms in the New World. They did not want a powerful nobility to develop so far away from home. In this manner, most Latin Americans of Hispanic descent lost this part of their heritage. I sometimes wonder if finding the coats of arms connected with their family trees would help young Latinos feel greater pride in this part of their heritage.

With our VW jam-packed with our belongings, Pat and I left Valladolid after a fascinating year. We were prepared to camp out in a small tent and wander through Europe for a month before taking a boat to New York. Over campfires while exploring back roads across Europe, we wondered if I had accomplished much teaching about U.S. history to students in that traditional community. You never really know for sure, but the thinking of some students was changed, I am sure.

I learned during our stay why a conservative dictator like Franco agreed to this liberal pilot program. It was the idea of one of his closest advisors, Manuel Fraga de Iribarne. This brilliant Gallego writer (Galicia is the northwest corner of Spain) and farsighted politician saw the need to educate a new generation of university students with knowledge about the world around them. He had persuaded the dictator to launch this educational program. Fraga was a conservative but practical fellow. He believed that you must know about everything around you and adjust to changing times to preserve what you have. One must be liberal to be conservative, he argued.

Southern France and Italy were very interesting, but ancient Greece made the biggest impression on us. It was a thrill to stand on the grassy field of the first Olympic games in 776 B.C., stroll around the temple at Delphi and the agora in Athens, and climb up to the Parthenon overlooking the city. All these places meant so much to me because I was teaching about them, based on my professors' lectures and books. Now I could teach from personal experience. At every campsite we spoke with neighbors who spoke English or Spanish. Our tent was so small that we could not spread out, but had to rotate to change positions. Campsites cost a dollar a night including showers and bathrooms.

Spain was the best place to camp or rest in cheap hotels. On one occasion, campsites were full because we goofed, driving until dark. We found a small hotel in a hilltop Spanish town. There was no one at the desk, and ringing the bell did no good. So, I took keys for a room from the rack, and we slept there that night. In the morning, there was still no one at the desk. We left the correct amount for the room in the mailbox and drove on.

We found our way to Belgium, where the enormous Queen Elizabeth ocean liner was waiting for the crossing to New York. A huge crane picked up our VW like a toy. It got washed from all angles to prevent bugs from entering the United States. We can't say that we enjoyed the crossing. I don't recommend a sea crossing of the Atlantic. It was stormy much of the way. We got cheated out of our room with a window to the outside, but it was too late to do anything about it. Our car and luggage were already on board. Poor Pat was already feeling the effects of pregnancy, and she had a hard time sleeping in our interior room.

One night, Pat went out for a short walk because she could not sleep due to her condition. The hallways were confusing, and on the way back she went into the wrong room. It was not me in bed but rather a stranger. Luckily, he did not wake up as she pulled back the blankets. She slipped out in terror and found our own room. The next morning when she told me about this, I burst out laughing and could barely stop. She got very mad because I thought it was so funny.

In New York, we simply drove our little car right off the boat and entered the city. Californian drivers have a reputation for recklessness, but they are saints compared to those in New York. People swear at each other and make obscene gestures, especially taxi drivers. We headed out as soon as we could identify a freeway heading anywhere to the west.

All across the country, we were so glad to be home and felt great pride in our vast America. For safety, we stayed in motels rather than camping out, as in Europe. As soon as we saw the Rocky Mountains in Colorado, we felt truly at home in the West.

We stayed with Pat's family until we found a house to

purchase close to the campus. The three-bedroom house on Rayen Street cost $14,000, with a down payment of $1,800. Pat was by now getting very large because she was carrying twins. We have a home movie of Carmen and Katie moving around inside as the doctor scanned Pat by some form of sound photography. Carmen and Katie were both eight pounds at birth and looked identical. Blood tests later revealed they were in effect half-identical. I didn't understand the medical explanation. They looked so much alike that for years Carmen cut her hair shorter so we could tell them apart. What a job it was: two of everything. I got up with Pat in the middle of the night for nursing and helped with what I could. Fortunately, the girls were remarkably good-natured, and still are.

Chapter 12

Founding a College in Bogotá

I had barely resumed teaching at Cal State Northridge when the girls were born. Another adventure soon came our way. The Great Lakes Colleges Association contracted me to found a new college for them somewhere in South America. I picked Bogotá, Colombia, and in a few months we took off for Bogotá with twin daughters six months old. Looking back, I would not do something like that again. I have always admired Pat agreeing to go along with this project and putting up with great inconveniences.

The twelve colleges in this group wanted a campus where they could send advanced students and professors to do research. Starting from scratch, I had to find a location, order several thousand basic reference books, hire staff, and outfit the building. I selected a very large house that preserved the colonial heritage. We remodeled it to suit our needs. Bogotá was outstanding in that it had about fifteen universities. It was possible to hire good local professors and staff. The American ambassador spoke at the inauguration of the campus, and many dignitaries showed up because El Centro de Estudios Universitarios Colombo-Americanos was unique.

One of the most interesting adventures while we were in Colombia was a field trip to the upper Amazon River basin. A Colombian military plane flew thirty students and staff to

Leticia on the Amazon River in a place you will never hear about. Our plane landed on a grass-covered field cut out from the jungle. We stayed for a week in a place where it seemed like time had stopped.

The Ticuna Indians there lived as they had five hundred years before. To be among them and see how they lived was worth a lot of book learning. Scary alligators, huge snakes, beautiful birds, and fish abounded. Although we were about 3,000 miles from its outlet in the Atlantic, the Amazon there was so wide you could not see the other side.

On a day-long boat tour we saw one Indian village after another. People were living just as they had when the Spanish and Portuguese explorers first saw them in the 1500s. Some of the Indians wore clothes due to Christian missionary pressure, but most did not. Few modern people wandered into this region when we were there. In later years, cocaine growers set up plantations in this area because it was so isolated. In time, this drug-growing activity and the introduction of money and social vices destroyed the traditional Indian lifestyle that we were fortunate to see before it disappeared. I regret that I did not have a video camera to record the life we saw there, but then, video cameras had not been invented at that time.

All of a sudden, Pat needed the best medical attention. She was infected by hepatitis, which kept her in bed for weeks. The girls were just walking when we decided to resign and come home after one year. Overall, going to Colombia was a mistake. The country was difficult for our style of family life. The students loved it, however, so the college lived on after we left. Pat remembers Colombia as the place that affected her thereafter, lowering her level of energy.

My department welcomed me back because such experiences only made me more valuable as a professor. Before long, I gained tenure. Such job security in the field of college teaching gives the professor freedom to think and express thoughts without fear of political consequences. It's a gamble for universities to grant tenure, but it benefits democratic, open societies. Every new idea must start in the mind of one person or a small group. Sometimes a minority point of view becomes accepted by the majority. In the play *Enemy of the People,* Norwegian Henrik Ibsen claimed that by the time the majority accepts a new idea, it is usually time for the minority group to think it over. As a member of a minority group, gaining tenure was a momentous event for me, for it expanded my freedom to speak out. I had job security.

Chapter 13

Entry into Politics in Los Angeles

Politics came into our family life unexpectedly. Politics was completely new to Pat. Her upbringing had not included the sort of experiences I had had in my youth with the Community Service Organization (CSO) in East Los Angeles. The CSO was an organization dedicated to empowering grassroots people in poor communities. Although Pat's family was of modest means, it was part of the American Anglo majority for whom everything was mostly just fine. My background was different. I had grown up knowing that political activism was necessary for survival and protection against discrimination.

My older brother Henry was a role model for me in politics. He was cofounder and succeeded the founding president Edward R. Roybal as head of the CSO. Roybal went on to become the first Mexican American elected to the Los Angeles City Council. This was truly a historic event because Mexican Americans faced many problems in becoming politically active. Campaign workers for Roybal had to be clever. To avoid the police, we had scouts posted a few blocks around as others nailed up Roybal posters on telephone posts. Although it was illegal, all candidates and parties advertised this way. But only Roybal workers were victims of police actions. These ranged from arrests to beatings. You can say that we were the "niggers" of California when blacks were still scarce in greater Los Angeles. The

CSO intended to change the way public life was conducted, and we were aware that our efforts were seen as threatening to the city and county political system.

Soon after the Second World War, Mexican-American political activism entered a new stage in southern California. Many social conditions were dismal in the barrios. These conditions were reflected by the under-performance of Mexican Americans in general life outside the barrios. There were no more than 50 Mexican-American students enrolled in UCLA out of about 20,000. As an indication of the progress made since about 1950, some 5,000 attended UCLA by the late 1990s. Similar progress took place all over the state and throughout the Southwest as well. By the year 2000, about 4,000 Mexican Americans were attending my university, CSUN, to which we could add the thousands in twenty other state university campuses in California. Access to higher education was only one of many handicaps that were overcome to reduce prejudice and expand opportunity for Mexican Americans. The progress has been enormous, although Spanish-surname students still fall far short of their number in the state universities proportionately.

Looking back, World War II veterans were called G.I.'s because everything they used was of government issue. Spanish-speaking G.I.'s came home as survivors and would not stomach the same old treatment. They had faced horrible conditions and dangers. Their new challenge was fitting into American society, which they saw with new eyes. They demanded to be called Mexican Americans, not just Mexicans. After their military experience, there was no doubt that they were as American as anyone else. I call this group of Mexican Americans the G.I. Generation. Life in the Southwest was changed by this generation of veterans. Although I was a younger member of the group, I felt like I was part of a new nationality. In many ways and in various places, this generation brought changes with national repercussions.

César Chávez, a young war veteran, was shaped by his early experience with the CSO. The Community Service Organization was founded by veterans of World War II. Fred Ross, who was a central figure in organizing the CSO, had a talent for identifying and recruiting people dedicated to social justice. He heard of César and brought him into the CSO, located in the barrio of East Los Angeles. In time, both César and Fred wanted the CSO to expand from an urban community service group to a rural one as well. The leadership of the CSO preferred to work in cities, so César and Fred left to help organize farmworkers. César became a national figure due to his dramatic struggle to unionize farmworkers and to protect them against pesticides used in agriculture, which were sometimes poisonous to farmworkers.

This short fellow was a giant in what he undertook. He survived threats against his life and led many religious processions on behalf of social justice in the fields. César used the ancient traditions of religious processions to include demonstrating for social justice and not just religion. Catholic, Protestant, and Jewish clergy often appeared together in these processions due to the common goals all three groups shared. Over the years, César went on fasts that lasted weeks, taking only water to drink and no food. His suffering was meant to draw attention to certain injustices. César's long fasts called national attention to farmworker needs, but damaged his health. I cannot imagine not eating for three weeks as he did.

Years later as I helped carry César's pine coffin down a long country road to a memorial service in the San Joaquin Valley, I recalled that César was just three months older than I. Other episodes in the life of the CSO passed through my mind as we marched down that road on that hot day. About 400,000 lined the road to the huge circus tent where notable people came from all over the country and abroad to pay their respects. Six men took turns carrying César's coffin on their shoulders, sweating in the hot sun. I wondered why he weighed so much. I finally guessed that a regular metal coffin was inside the pine one, hence the weight. Many men took turns as we moved slowly along silent crowds. I was on the left side of the coffin and later moved to the front on the right side and back again. The weight hurt one's shoulder, but I helped carry César for more than my turn because I figured I would do a turn for Henry as well. I treasure the picture a friend took of that occasion.

Reverend Jesse Jackson, the black civil rights leader, came with bodyguards and insisted on walking just behind the coffin. This was resented, and so dark Mexican farmworkers stepped in behind César's coffin. The reverend's group soon found itself fifty feet back. Los Angeles Cardinal Roger Mahoney presided over the ceremonies, and members of the Kennedy family attended, among other dignitaries.

In the midst of this revival of political activism, our tree-covered backyard lent itself to rallies and fundraisers. Our twin girls were growing up and gradually understood why hundreds of strangers would be in the backyard on occasion. They were always a showpiece because they looked so much alike. Pat did not like all this political activity, but I explained that good things do not happen by themselves. In time, she came to accept it, although she never liked it.

In 1967, our son Julian Paul was born, to round out our family with three children. I was and am so happy to have a son to carry on my family name. And, both Carmen and Katie have chosen to follow the Hispanic custom of keeping their father's paternal name and simply adding the family names of their husbands. The year 1967 was important in another respect. I gained election to the Los Angeles Board of Education and started a political career.

Chapter 14

Twelve Years on the Los Angeles School Board

In 1965, the first black person was elected to the Los Angeles Board of Education. A liberal coalition had come together to accomplish this major upset in local ethnic politics. The coalition was made up of West Los Angeles Jews, citywide Anglo liberals, blacks, and Mexican Americans. This political feat was significant because the school district included all of Los Angeles City and twelve connected cities in the huge urban basin stretching from the mountains to the sea. Since each of the seven board members was elected at large, they were elected from the district as a whole. Each school board member was elected by more people than the mayor of Los Angeles, the county supervisor, or our members of congress. Reverend James Jones had been elected to the school board in an area represented by twelve members of congress. A finer man could not have joined the school board.

The same coalition then turned to electing the first Mexican American to the school board in 1966. To avoid divisions and maximize strength, the crosstown coalition asked the Mexican-American leadership to identify one consensus candidate whom the coalition could support in 1967.

It was a challenge how this could be done in light of the many competing groups in the Mexican-American barrios of greater Los Angeles. Learning from the black experience and pressured by members of the liberal coalition, Mexican-American leaders came to a unique agreement. To satisfy the request of the crosstown allies, barrio leaders formed the Congress of Mexican-American Unity. Such a convention set out to select a candidate, just like national party conventions did. Each of ninety-two Mexican-American organizations that joined the congress chose their voting delegates based on the recorded number of their members.

I was persuaded to throw my hat into the ring as a candidate, despite it being late in the preconvention activity. My supporters had a plan to overcome my late entry as a candidate. This involved hundreds of phone calls to delegates beforehand. The convention in December 1966 was a lot of fun, filled with banners, parades, and partisan cheers. The speeches from many candidates went on for hours. Only soft drinks were available, and the whole thing was pretty much like a party. The Congress of Mexican-American Unity was a unique event in Mexican-American history.

Thanks to the help of many volunteers, I barely beat out the front-runner, Professor Manuel Guerra of the University of Southern California. There were loud demands for a recount, but my election was confirmed. Manuel still charged fraud, and broke the candidates' pledge by running for the office anyway. In spring 1967, the campaign began. Using the tactics and organizational methods of Reverend Jones's campaign, we set out to work in the huge electoral district.

Pat had very serious reservations about my running for public office. Before the nominating convention, I had told her that Manuel would get the nomination anyway, so there was no harm done in being a candidate. When I was proven wrong on the first prediction, I told her not to worry. No Mexican American had ever won such a region-wide race in this century. Even if elected, against all odds, I told her I would never get reelected. When she asked why, I replied that I would do what I thought was best for everyone's children, not just Mexican Americans. Moreover, I would speak out on public matters, regardless of whether my views were popular or not. This would not be well received by various groups for different reasons. How wrong I was in each case.

The incumbent officeholder was a good man but very conservative. Unfortunately for his candidacy, he said in public that Mexican-American children were poor academic students because they were just lazy. He was a good target for someone who was experienced in public speaking and could respond to such distortions. University lecturing, in addition to the CSO experience, had prepared me very well to speak to all groups across town.

The number and quality of volunteers in the school board race were impressive. Some volunteers stood out, such as Morrie Weiner, who was attached to the Los Angeles mayor's office, and Joe Roos of the Jewish Pentagon, as everyone called the headquarters of the American Jewish Committee. Reverend Jones recruited prominent blacks. Among Mexican Americans, supporters in labor unions were especially helpful. The major teacher organizations also worked hard for us. The many graduates of Roosevelt High School were an unexpected resource. Countless graduates rallied to help just because I was a fellow "Rough Rider." The multiracial and multiethnic student body of Roosevelt High School had built up a spirit of brotherhood among all graduates. The moment someone you met found out you were also a Rough Rider, you were a pal.

Charles Reed Smoot got the largest number of the votes in the primary election, but not an absolute majority. That is, more people voted for someone else than for him. He was in trouble. The historical record showed that candidates like him lost in the runoff election when paired off against just one opponent.

The runoff was fun because now everyone on our side felt optimistic. It was also significant that Professor Manuel Guerra did poorly in the primary election, dropped out of civic life, and moved to another state. More help sprang up everywhere. More Mexican Americans registered to vote, Presbyterian voters turned out in larger numbers, thanks to my brother-in-law, Reverend Tony Hernández. As a Presbyterian minister, he spread the gospel among the Spanish-speaking congregations, like Reverend Martin Luther King did among black congregations. Fellow graduates of East Los Angeles public schools, such as Roosevelt High School and East Los Angeles Junior College, rallied to the cause. After an upset election that was noted across the country, I took the oath of office in June 1967. Pat was both proud and worried about the effect on our children.

My election tipped the balance on the board to the liberal side. Mexican-American communities across the country took notice of this political event and were stimulated to increase their local civic activity. Before long, I was invited to speak all over the Southwest, and farther away as well. Some Democratic party leaders wondered what office I would run for next, and public relations companies offered to represent me to promote a public image by arranging my speaking engagements and appearances in many places that were not related to education. Perhaps it was a mistake, but I turned down these offers. There is no telling where this might have led me.

Television cameras broadcast school board meetings regularly because education was on everyone's mind. The civil rights struggles of the 1960s were in full force, and now minority groups were in a position to make changes in the nation's second-largest school district. Presbyterian Reverend Jones and I soon sponsored numerous changes, which our two other liberal board members supported. Just as often as us, UCLA Professor Ralph Richardson and Georgiana Hardy came up with good ideas, which had previously gone down to defeat. Los Angeles and New York public schools set patterns for the rest of the country. Los Angeles school board member remarks were often quoted far away, as well as at home.

Board members each had a chauffeured private car with a telephone. Our children thought this was amazing. Car phones were very new at the time. The driver would take board members anywhere anytime, so that we could cover the massive area for school visits and community meetings. Board meeting days on Mondays and Thursdays started early and ended in the evening. This was hard on Pat because she had to care for the children alone much of the time. I was still a full-time professor at the university. Visiting schools across the huge district took a lot of time. I was busy all week and weekends as well. I always came home tired.

I soon made it clear by my actions and public statements that I was not just a Mexican-American school board member. I was there to serve all the children whose parents had elected me. This annoyed some Mexican-American folks, but I asked them to avoid discrimination in reverse. I stated many times in our barrios that rarely could we hope to elect anyone to public office with only Mexican-American votes. If an elected official avoided favoring his own group, this would earn support outside our group for other Mexican-American candidates.

My election was part of an awakening among Mexican Americans across the country. Mexican-American college students were becoming increasingly active in their struggle for equality and acceptance of their Mexican culture. They learned from black activism, but preserved some special qualities peculiar to our historical experience. Bilingual and bicultural characteristics of Mexican Americans were at the heart of their feelings, and César Chávez was their role model.

The war in Vietnam was dividing the nation, and President Lyndon B. Johnson was fighting on two fronts: the Vietnam War abroad and the war on poverty at home. The combination was exhausting our national resources. Our involvement in Vietnam was forcing high school youths to take sides on a war for which they were soon to be drafted. In the barrios we all knew about casualty rates among Mexican Americans. Blacks and Mexican Americans tended to be in the front lines. Postwar data revealed that Mexican Americans were once again, as in World War II and Korea, the most decorated single ethnic group. This was a source of pride, but anger as well.

A very historic meeting took place in October of 1967. President Johnson convened cabinet-level hearings on Mexican Americans in El Paso. Nothing quite like this had ever happened before. Most Americans did not know that President Johnson had been raised in a poor neighborhood of southern Texas and had taught in a segregated "Mexican school." He knew Mexican Americans and experienced firsthand that education was the key to their progress. Experts from all over the country presented papers on all aspects of Mexican-American life. Such a collection of experts had never been gathered before. Since I had just been elected to a prominent office in Los Angeles County, it was easy for others to assume that I knew more than I did. I spoke on public education. As a matter of fact, I knew as much as most attendees and more than many of them.

All the members of the president's cabinet were present among the large turnout of invitees. This meeting brought together Mexican activists as well. The presentations were later published and are found in major libraries. The mailing list of attendees proved to be invaluable because now new relationships between Mexican-American leaders were formed.

The president soon appointed a special assistant in the White House for Mexican-American affairs. Vicente Ximenes undertook the gigantic task of encouraging cabinet departments to help Mexican Americans. No other group had ever enjoyed such White House distinction.

At an educational conference late one night in Albuquerque, I was enjoying refreshments and good company with Mexican-American friends. Professor George Sánchez explained the origins of all this presidential attention. It turns out that President Johnson and George had grown up together in a poor town in Texas and shared schooling all the way through college. George was the better student, and he always helped Lyndon with schoolwork. In time, their paths parted. Lyndon started teaching in a segregated Mexican school, and George went on to graduate school, becoming a distinguished professor of Spanish and author of the first major work on American Hispanics. *Forgotten People* can be called a pathfinder work, for it was the first of a kind.

After the assassination of President John F. Kennedy in 1963, Johnson occupied the White House. George phoned the president to congratulate his old friend, but Johnson's secretary would not put George through to the president. Each president has a list of people that can be put through to him whenever they call. George politely informed the lady that if she did not inform the president that his old friend George Sánchez was on the line, she would be scolded for sure. The secretary had probably learned already about LBJ's temper and use of profanity. After a short wait, George said he heard the president shout through the phone, "Jorge, where have you been keeping yourself, you sonofabitch?" George replied, "Hiding in New Mexico from my ex-wife who is after my hide." After a roaring laugh, the president asked what he could do for George. George suggested a national conference to come up with ways to help his people. The president understood what his old friend meant and quietly asked George to contact a certain White House aide, who would do whatever George recommended. George made many demands for the El Paso conference, and the presidential aides just smiled and complied, he told us.

The novelty of my election produced invitations to speak all over the country, and I accepted as many as I could. School people assumed I knew more than I did, and this made me uncomfortable until I accepted the fact that at least I knew more about helping Mexican-American children in school than they did. I traveled to Washington state, Wyoming, Idaho, Oregon, and other states where Mexican-American children were now becoming numerous. New York educators were surprised that I could give advice on Puerto Rican children until I told them about living in Puerto Rico, Spain, Venezuela, and Colombia. Hispanic-surnamed folks vary greatly in their appearance, speech, and customs, but there is a common base. Educators are often confused by differences among Hispanics and were starting to ask for help from folks like me.

The 1960s were very tumultous years. The war in Vietnam was dividing the country more bitterly all the time. Television reporting brought the gory details of the war into everyone's living room. This war was the first that civilians at home could see in living color. Thousands of young men were running away to places like Mexico and Canada because they refused to fight in what they believed was a senseless and unjust war. Civil rights issues also divided the nation as minority groups tried to get laws passed and court judgments to eliminate prejudice based on race. Many thousands of demonstrators marched in cities across the nation, and sometimes riots broke out. Police occasionally used violence to break up some of these demonstrations, but they could do little when various American cities suffered huge fires set by angry, disaffected mobs.

The FBI drew up lists of people involved in making demands for justice, because some people feared we were near a civil war. I know I was on some of these lists. I asked for a copy of the FBI file on me, thanks to a new law that gave citizens that right. It took almost a year before the file was mailed to me. Many lines of the file were blacked out in secrecy. During these years the FBI was worried that the French Canadian desire for independence from Canada might be adopted by Mexican Americans. Black Americans did not pose such a threat, but then Mexico was only next door and not across the Atlantic. I sometimes wonder whether I should ask for a copy of the most recent file, if only to see how long I was under surveillance as a Chicano activist.

The Civil Rights Act of 1965 was enacted by Congress, and President Lyndon B. Johnson signed it in a major ceremony. He had pushed it strongly to the point of alienating many white people in the South, as well as elsewhere. I don't know if President Johnson could predict that traditional Democrats in the southern states would soon swing to the Republican Party, which was less enthusiastic about civil rights. To his credit, LBJ overcame opposition in Congress to gain passage of this act. This shift in political power, prompted by the civil rights issue, changed the national balance of power thereafter.

After joining the school board, like Don Quixote, I began giving modest college scholarships to Mexican-American youths. This noble gesture could not make a major impact on the problem, although it made me feel better that some young people were getting help, thanks to my school board income. Pat reminded me that these scholarships meant that, in effect, I was serving on the school board for free. To save for our own children's future, we eventually stopped the Nava scholarships.

I was able to help with scholarships in another manner. Vicki Carr was in her singing glory during this time. She sang beautifully in English and Spanish. Every year, Vicki had been taking on the costs of a complete college education of a Mexican-American boy or girl through graduate school, if need be. I thought she was an angel, as well as a great singer. I suggested she set up a foundation that could gather money to add to what she donated. That was the origin of the Vicki Carr Foundation. Before long, many donors were contributing to the Vicki Carr Scholarship Fund.

About this time, my good friend Edward Moreno came up with the idea of forming a national scholarship fund for Mexican Americans, like the United Negro College Fund. We learned through the grapevine that others were thinking of the same idea, especially in Miami (mostly Cubans), New York (Puerto Ricans), and Texas (Mexican Americans). Since none of the other groups had someone like a school board member at the helm of their group, they agreed with Edward's proposal that we join efforts. We met on neutral ground, and, in spite of my misgivings, a Texan Catholic priest served as referee to smooth over the rivalry. This led to the formation of the National Hispanic Scholarship Fund, which has grown steadily over the years. By the turn of the century, it had given away several hundred thousand dollars annually after a modest start of about $12,000 the first year.

When I took over the U.S. embassy in Mexico in 1980, President Jimmy Carter insisted that his ambassadors resign from all groups in order to avoid even the appearance of conflicts of interest. Upon my return from Mexico, the foundation did not invite me to be a member of the board again, even though I had been a founder. I was surprised and offended, leading me to look back and find whether there was a basis for this rejection. The rejection reflected the domination of the National Hispanic Scholarship Fund by the Catholic church and a reaction against my strategy for fundraising, as best I could figure.

For years, some Protestant and Catholic leaders sought ways to promote cooperation between all the churches that were Christian. Such a coming together of all Christian churches promised to reduce rivalry among the various branches of Christianity. Some Catholics believed that the ecumenical movement threatened the historical authority of the Pope. During these years, while paying lip service to it publicly, the Pope was discouraging the ecumenical movement. This practice meant that Catholics in an ecumenical group should try to gain control of it. In the event they could not gain control, it was better to leave the group. I learned about this unofficial practice from my brother-in-law, who was a Presbyterian minister, and saw it practiced firsthand. I regretted such narrow thinking, but supported the scholarship fund because it did such good work.

Bypassing me for reappointment to the board may well have come from other sources, however. By now I was becoming radical in some of my thinking. I tried to get the governing board of the National Hispanic Scholarship Fund to adopt aggressive ways to get more funds. Our polite fundraising was negligible compared to the need. I suggested that scholarship funds buy a few stocks to obtain financial reports of companies doing major business in the barrios. Such research could be conducted by scholarship recipients as part of their regular college studies. When major businesses earned millions of dollars a year from sales to barrio customers, we could strongly urge them to give back a share to the community and get good publicity as well.

As a product of public life, I overheard from donors that their multimillion-dollar firms gave only several thousand dollars a year for community groups. Although these donors bragged about their generosity, their donations were peanuts, frankly. I figured that through public disclosures of indifference to their customers, and even consumer boycotts, if necessary, many millions could be gained for our educational needs. I was not able to arouse support for such a plan. Bishop Patrick Flores, the gentle advisor to the National Hispanic Scholarship Fund, rejected the pressure tactics that I suggested. Maybe that explained the cooling off in our relations by the time I went to Mexico as U.S. ambassador.

I could have been wrong, of course. But in the early 1970s, federal data showed that Hispanic consumers spent about $30 billion per year. This was now being called the Hispanic market. I saw this as social power. Just one-tenth of 1 percent of these sales assigned to scholarships would be about $30 million per year, all tax deductible. I thought that big business owed this to the community. The need to cement corporate giving was all the more vital as I saw the pattern of increasing foreign ownership of American firms. Boards of directors abroad would care even less than Americans for our barrios. I argued that we must establish a precedent and not be bashful about our goals.

Ernest Robles, cofounder and president of the foundation until he retired, was successful in raising more funds annually. My daughter Carmen, years later, received one of the grants to complete her doctorate at UCLA, following her father as a professor of history.

Chapter 15

The East Los Angeles Walkouts in 1968

Within a year of my election to the Los Angeles Board of Education, the school district exploded into turmoil as thousands of Mexican-American students simply walked out of high schools. The students paraded down the streets protesting against inferior education and discrimination. The walkouts of 1968 made history because no such mass protest by high school students had ever taken place before. Furthermore, the walkouts were conducted by Mexican-American young people who had never behaved in this manner.

The Los Angeles police and the school district police worked together and soon discovered that a high school teacher at Lincoln High School was advising the students. Sal Castro was a very popular teacher at Lincoln High School because he inspired students to study and struggle for justice. I knew Sal well because he had worked in my election campaign less than a year earlier. He may not have been the best teacher, when measured by traditional standards used by the school district; however, he inspired students and they loved him.

He was an inspiration, no doubt, as students paraded in the streets of East Los Angeles with placards and sang protest songs fully in the American tradition. Unlike social protest demonstrations in other cities, the young Mexican-American students caused no harm to public property. In fact, I saw some proud old-timers on the sidewalks cheering the students as they passed. Sal was teaching the students things you don't learn in books. In my view he was a hero.

The walkouts produced a serious split between the student leadership and me as school board member. The students were protesting against the same conditions and educational attitudes that I had denounced during the campaign. However, the students were taking matters into their own hands and were in violation of state law. Some of these young people saw me as one of the school district establishment. Through their eyes filled with passion, many saw an enemy in me. Their impressions were confirmed in part when hundreds of them stormed into the public sessions of the school board. Among the students, I spotted some old-timers I knew to be radical leftists, if not communists. When my eyes met one of the protesters who had worked on my election campaign, I mouthed out silently, "you bastard," and he looked away embarrassed.

Overflow crowds were turned away from the auditorium by police as the school board tried to cope with the unique situation. TV cameras were broadcasting live across the country as these beautiful young people saw their first Mexican-American school board member in action. While most of the young people were polite, all of them were very excited. Some were rowdy, and others were shouting vulgar language at the school board even though it was trying to understand their concerns. In contrast to student expectations, I was respectful and used reasoning to help my colleagues resolve the heated issues. What was worse than that for some of the protesters, I had to compromise to get some of what I wanted approved by the school board.

Black school board member Reverend Jones and I were in the same situation in this respect. Black protesters criticized him for not producing all the results they sought since his election two years earlier. High school students were acting on emotion rather than reason. This was not bad in itself, but it made dealing with the walkouts very difficult. I was proud of these student protesters, while also very angry with those who were aggravating the discussions by rude conduct.

After two years of hard work, two of my books on Mexican-American history for public schools were about to appear in print as the walkouts broke out. In an ironic coincidence, they were the very first such books published in the United States. This did not help to prove my concern for Mexican-American students. To mention this form of dedication on my part would have been like spitting into the wind. Many students were inspired by their leaders to call me an Oreo—that is, brown on the outside while white on the inside.

The East L.A. Walkouts made Sal Castro a hero to many people. However, school district officials and the police saw him as a dangerous agitator. I spoke to Sal Castro from a public phone on one occasion and alerted him to what was in store. Law enforcement was organizing to put down this student revolt, and he was a major target. I told him that the school board would have fired him except for my pleading on his behalf, but I was not sure he believed me. I alerted Sal to be very careful in what he said and did because he was being followed and taped. He laughed and said that he had stopped using his telephone at home some time ago. I confessed I phoned him from a public phone also because I feared that my phones were tapped. Fortunately, I was on good terms with the school district security staff. Indirect remarks by a friend in security had led me to take such precautions. Sometimes, in fact, I made misleading remarks on the office phone that I wanted recorders to hear. I played my games, too.

Before long, Sal's teaching was interrupted by his arrest. Although he was released on bail, his trial went on for some time, as he was kept busy doing nothing at the central school board headquarters. He could have been found guilty of a misdemeanor but Los Angeles District Attorney Evelle Younger chose to charge him with conspiracy, which is a felony. A felony conviction could earn him years in prison. The felony charge was that Sal had conspired to commit a misdemeanor! The reasoning was that to spit on the sidewalk is a misdemeanor, but to conspire with someone to spit on the sidewalk is a felony. After a lengthy trial in which he was defended by bright, young Mexican-American lawyers wrestling with the legal giants of the city, Sal was found innocent. Sal Castro will be a hero for the rest of his life.

In reality, the walkouts actually made it easier for me to get more things done, because now the board could see the alternative to educational reform. Fortunately for everyone, the school board was made up of intelligent, thoughtful, and understanding people.

Right after the walkouts, the school board devised a handy way to hear students and members of the community who wanted to speak on educational issues. The board convened symbolically at Lincoln High School where the walkouts had started. Fortunately, its auditorium was among the largest in the school district. Each speaker was granted five minutes. About a hundred speakers of all ages gave the board an earful. All told, the staff counted ninety-two demands for improvement of education in Los Angeles schools. Many of the demands were beneficial for all students, actually. Listening to presentations in English and Spanish took away much of the heat of the walkouts. I still have a sound recording of that famous session. In any case, students returned to their four high schools as heroes. The walkouts also produced a "sleep-in" at the Los Angeles

Board of Education auditorium. This was unheard of, comical, and productive. Mexican-American parents had hastily formed a grassroots organization called the Educational Issues Reform Committee in order to demonstrate support for their children's crusade and to pressure the school board by showing family support for the young people.

I can still recall the scene. For the allotted five minutes, Reverend Vahac Mardirosian addressed the school board backed by cheers from the packed auditorium. He ended by stating with a minister's solemnity that the community would wait until the school board responded to their requests for reform. The board president calmly replied that it would take a week for a reply to be shaped. Reverend Mardirosian calmly announced that the community would wait there for a reply. Men and women from the barrios of East Los Angeles camped out in the auditorium until the school board met again. Night and day they slept in the chairs and on the floor. Only children were sent home, but the adults remained, and the school district was wise enough to not eject them. When the school board replied a week later to the demands, some three hundred folks left the auditorium calmly, as well as neat and clean. You could not tell they had been there. When the youthful protesters saw their parents and neighbors stand up for them, the classes filled up again. Also, some communist-leaning barrio guys had little to take advantage of after this display of family unity and democracy in action.

The questionable example of walking out of schools in Los Angeles was imitated in other southwestern schools. The East L.A. Walkouts of 1968 became a central part of Chicano mythology. Stories about them, partly true and partly not true, emerged as participants reported on them from their points of view. School principals and teachers in Los Angeles who had opposed the walkouts were ordered to establish a new understanding with the peaceful rebels. After high school and college graduation, many of these rebels became teachers, lawyers, film producers, and other professionals in later years. I have smiled at this because their turn came to join some establishment and then have to work as a member of a team. I have sometimes wondered if my moderate conduct seemed wiser to these youthful radicals as they grew older.

Chapter 16

THE CHICANO MOVEMENT

What groups call themselves defines what is in their hearts and minds. In the 1960s, Mexican-American young people began calling themselves "Chicanos" and soon insisted that all Mexican Americans do the same. Among the college and high school youths of this decade, "Chicano" was replacing "Mexican American" among the majority population as well. Where did this term come from? No one planned it; it just got started and spread like a brushfire fed by new magazines and circulars printed by Mexican-American youths. About the same time, American blacks replaced the label "Negro." I didn't like "Chicano" because I knew that it was slang in Mexico for a low-class person. Most people of my generation felt as I did about the new label. In the face of youthful insistence, only gradually did older Mexican Americans say, "Okay, okay, I'm Chicano."

Students insisted at university and public meetings on the use of "Chicano" as a sign of pride in one's heritage. Refusing to use the term labeled you an "Oreo." Calling you a cookie that is brown on the outside but is white on the inside meant you were a traitor to your group. Anglos and others adopted "Chicano" just as they had "black" over "Negro." I had no choice but to call myself a Chicano, too. I still prefer "Mexican American," however, because it is clearer.

Militant pride in being Chicano was accompanied by a revival in pride for Mexican roots, especially Aztec Indian roots. Since I knew enough about ancient Mexican history, I found it hard to admire the Aztecs as the Chicano generation did. The Spaniards arriving in Mexico City for the first time were amazed by Aztec civilization, which they soon realized included poetry, literature, music, and complicated economics. However, the Aztecs were hated by nearby Indian peoples, whom they had conquered and exploited brutally. Speaking to community groups, I failed in many efforts to divert admiration from the Aztecs to earlier Zapotec, Mayan, and other Indian cultures that had actually served as a foundation for Aztec culture. Chicanos claimed to be descendants of Aztecs for better or worse.

In popular movements, it seems that when a belief takes hold, nothing can change it. The idea gains a life of its own. This sort of mythology became a vital part of the Chicano movement during the 1960s. The Chicano generation ignored their G.I. parents, who had tried to gain an identification as American. Chicanos instead defined themselves vaguely in bicultural and binational terms, which included hostility to American culture.

These were complicated times. The Vietnam War was costing more and more American lives. Poorer Americans had fewer opportunities to gain exemption from military service by attending college, so they could not avoid the military draft. Chicanos and blacks represented a part of our fighting forces much beyond their percentage of the population. This overrepresentation meant more casualties. Curiously, young Chicanos and blacks did not join the ranks of young Anglo-Americans fleeing to Canada or Europe to avoid military service. If their number came up for service, Chicanos put on the uniform. Once again in Vietnam, as in Korea and World War II, Spanish-surnamed soldiers were the most decorated group for valor. This was something to be proud of, and folks in the barrios were aware of it.

This period was complicated by not only urban unrest over the war and civil rights, but also by farmworker strikes and boycotts led by César Chávez. Furthermore, the efforts of French-speaking Canadians to form their own country complicated matters. While violence was avoided, Canada seemed to be splitting apart due to French-Canadian demands. Canada's plight raised fears about Chicano youths, some of whom spoke often about Aztlán. This was the Aztec term for their homeland, extending perhaps as far north as the American Southwest. When Chicano leaders like Corky Gonzales of Colorado called for a rebirth of Aztlán in the Southwest, this seemed like a call for secession to frightened white conservatives from coast to coast. Corky's lengthy poem, *I am Joaquín,* thrilled us but frightened others. Corky referred to Chicanos as heirs to Aztlán, the mythical home of the Aztecs in the American Southwest. From here, they had migrated south to Mexico and built an empire, he claimed.

From the White House of Richard Nixon down to local law enforcement, all this Aztlán stuff and street demonstrating mustered images of the type of separatism the French Canadians or the American confederates had wanted. The spread of bilingual education added to the anxiety among some people. Chicanos adopted the blacks' use of terms such as "Black Power" by referring to "Brown Power." Since some blacks were very belligerent and even violent, Chicanos were painted with the same brush. They appeared as a threat to the fabric of society and national unity. Looking back, Chicanos were gentle revolutionaries, but got little credit for their manners.

The idea of separating the Chicano population from the American cultural mainstream led to the formation of the La

Raza Unida political party. Some Chicano activists denounced both the Republican and Democratic parties as indifferent to minority needs. The Raza Unida party sought to undermine the political monoply of the two-party system.

In several states the Raza Unida Party ran its own candidates for public office though with only modest success. Just the same, the political movement seemed like an effort to destroy the traditional political party structure. It never was. I turned down offers to join the party and remained a Democrat. This only served to alienate other Chicanos from my approach to improving our conditions by working within the system.

In both California and Texas, Chicano groups tried to establish their own colleges and universities. As a university professor, my involvement and support was attractive to some organizers, but I let them down by refusing to support the idea. I failed to persuade some leaders of this effort that it was ill-fated. The obstacles to building a library and hiring staff—especially qualified professors—were overwhelming. Although Congress and southern states annually appropriated many millions of dollars to support black colleges, universities, and professional schools, Chicanos did not have the political power to gain such support. Why condemn well-intentioned students to a second-class degree at best, when we could make better use of already established public universities supported by public funds, including our tax contributions? I failed to convince some Chicano leaders that my lack of enthusiasm for Chicano colleges did not mean lack of concern for the general goal. I lost some friends due to this, but then maybe they were not real friends.

Law enforcement at the federal and state levels drew up lists of Chicanos to place in jail without trial, if matters became too unsettled. Such a measure was to be called "detention," just like the Japanese-American "relocation" into desert camps after Pearl Harbor. How do I know this? Former California Attorney General Evelle Younger told me about these plans years later. We were sitting in his living room as fellow members of the board of directors of the Pacific Coast Branch of the U.S.-Mexico Chamber of Commerce. Younger was apologetic about all this, for by now he had realized that all this establishment hysteria was uncalled for. Evelle had been the Los Angeles district attorney who prosecuted Sal Castro with much vehemence some years earlier. Formerly political opponents, we were now friends. He took pains to tell me about his early family poverty that matched mine and how he and his wife struggled to buy their modest home in West Los Angeles.

I never got involved in the La Raza Unida Party because I felt it was counterproductive. Such a political move would raise fears about us and make it harder to work with establishment groups. The Democratic Party was our best political ally. Therefore, we had to try to enlarge our influence in this party, in spite of its faults. Among these faults was favoring black political demands over ours. The civil rights movement was a national movement involving the redress of injustice to blacks, and rightly so. The Chicano movement was known only in the southwestern part of the nation, and even then in a distorted manner.

During the 1960s and 1970s, the California Republican Party made greater efforts to enlist Mexican Americans. They reached a high point of about 30 percent of Mexican-American voters. Men like Dr. Francisco Bravo made substantial monetary contributions to Ronald Reagan's campaign for governor of California and enjoyed some financial benefits from this. State contracts for public health care were assigned to his clinic. Bravo urged me strongly to join other Mexican Americans who were jumping over the fence to the Republican side. I declined the impassioned offer and remained a member of the Democratic Party.

But I was proud about all this Chicano activity, for I was part of it. My election to the Los Angeles Board of Education in 1967 stimulated the Chicano movement in California. We will never know the full extent, but the East Los Angeles Walkouts took place just eight months after I took office, and most of the early Chicano movement leaders in southern California had been associated with my election. The election was reflected by increased political activity up and down the state and in other states as well. At that time, not a single Mexican American was elected to the state legislature, and only Edward R. Roybal was a member of Congress from this area. This underrepresentation ended gradually as a product of the Chicano movement, which stimulated broad political involvement by Mexican Americans.

This new era was exciting, to say the least. Those of us in different areas of activity sometimes disagreed over the goals we should seek and methods to use. Shouting sessions were common, and many friendships dissolved as new ones formed. I recall one shouting match with Sal Castro over the phone in which he took me to task for going along with moderate reform measures of the school board. I replied that half a loaf was better than none and that with time we would get the other half. I also reminded him that as right as I might be, I needed three other votes on the board to make up a majority. "Sal," I shouted, "you are lucky a moderate like me is on the board. The police and the district administration still want to crucify you. I don't know how long I can hold them off. Just don't put anything in writing, use public phones, and don't trust anyone you don't know well."

As it turned out, the worst punishment he got was a transfer to another high school away from Lincoln High, where most students loved him. Many of his fellow teachers wanted to lynch him, however, and were delighted when he was transferred.

Years after the walkouts ended, black and Chicano activism continued to alarm many people in the state and national governments. I was always careful about what I said and did in order to avoid becoming a casualty. I was also aware that I was a role model. After all, so much work had been done to elect me to that vital post that I was watchful not to spoil the effects of the gains. Evelle Younger and I talked about the walkouts and Chicano activism at great length on several occasions. He told me that there was real fear over black and Chicano activism. It seemed like the United States was being invaded. I jokingly told him not to worry: Mexican Americans also opposed undocumented Mexican workers, except for their cousins.

In addition to fear about Mexican Americans, destructive black riots in several cities and the activities of white protesters, such as Tom Hayden, who had disrupted the Democratic Party national convention in Chicago, made civil war appear a possibility. Paid troublemakers were used by the FBI to harm both black and Chicano groups that sought reforms. These guys came from barrios and looked and acted like ordinary Mexican Americans. These government spies joined community groups and reported on their activities. At times, they became troublemakers by promoting activities that would get the groups into trouble with the law. Surveillance of Chicano leaders was common, and telephones were tapped in more cases than we know about. Some of the FBI agents later went public and confessed to their activities.

The role of the Brown Berets in the Southwest provides a good example of police tactics used to discredit genuine reformers. The Brown Berets were healthy and idealistic young men in East Los Angeles who were imitating their relatives fighting in special units in Vietnam. The young men designed brown uniforms, wore brown berets, and practiced military-style drills. Intense discipline was a feature of their ethos. The Brown Berets were organized to help the community by fighting drug traffic and juvenile delinquency. They sponsored activities for youth. They were also outspoken critics of political injustices. All this made them appear threatening to power groups in education and politics.

The military bearing of the Brown Berets made the FBI go after them as a dangerous regional group. But harassment by the authorities only made the young people intensify their discipline and energies.

After one school board meeting, a district security official, who shall remain anonymous, whispered that the police were going to raid the Brown Beret headquarters that night in search of drugs. That's all he said. I got to a public phone right away to call David Sánchez, the handsome young commander of the Brown Berets. I had usually been criticized by the Berets because I could not bring about as many changes in the school system as they wanted. To most Brown Berets, I was an Oreo. I could understand their point of view, but it did hurt my feelings. There I was on the school board, trying to get three other votes for some measure, while the Brown Beret youngsters were glowering at me as a "sellout." I wanted to give them *un abrazo* (a hug) instead. Thoughts like these crossed my mind as I went to see David.

David met me on the sidewalk on Soto Street, just north of the malt shop at the corner with Brooklyn Avenue. Luther was my school board driver, a large and wonderful black friend who loved horses, as did the Navas. I had told Luther what I was up to, and somehow he got me to Brooklyn and Soto in five minutes, keeping the engine running as I spoke to David. I told David about the raid that could take place any minute and then sped off with Luther.

By the time the police arrived minutes later, the young people had turned their offices inside out and found a plastic bag with drugs inside the toilet water tank. The drugs were flushed down the toilet as the police streamed in. The police tore up the offices without a search warrant and destroyed as much as they could out of anger that the drugs were not where they had been planted. But who had planted them? It had to be a Brown Beret.

Among the most important reforms that came from the walkouts was the formation of school advisory councils to enlarge the role of the Parent Teacher Associations (PTAs). Rather than simply include parents, the Community Advisory Councils (CACs) were to include all elements from the community served by a particular school. In the case of high schools, the school board hoped that future employers would participate in the CACs in order to help schools prepare young people for specific jobs.

Before long, schools changed as CACs made recommendations on curriculum, teaching methods, and other elements of school life. CACs could only make recommendations to the principal, and when a stalemate took place, they could bring their views to the entire school board in a public session. Minority schools particularly went through considerable transformation.

A long process had only just begun. For twelve years, school board life dominated Nava family life. I arranged my class schedule at the university to allow for school board committees and board meetings. Pat and the children missed seeing me those two days, but we tried to make the other time together worthwhile.

Chapter 17

Leveraging the School Board Position Nationally

Lecturing and consulting on Mexican-American education took considerable time during the twelve years on the school board. From coast to coast, school districts as well as universities invited me to speak because there were few experts on Mexican Americans. Although no one knows everything even today, I guess I knew about as much as anyone else in view of personal experiences and involvement in Mexican-American affairs. What gave me additional authority in the eyes of others was the enormous size of my electoral district and the high regard for the Los Angeles school system.

My visit to Wyoming was typical of these lecture tours. Wyoming was the land of the Marlboro cigarette ads with blond cowboys on horseback. These highway billboards were a fraud, I learned in Laramie. The sons of cattle ranchers no longer wanted to ride the range year-round. The ranchers fattened cattle on thousands of acres they leased from the federal government for next to nothing. Even then, these folks were always Republicans and argued against big government and federal grants to minority groups, ignoring their own benefits that were far older and more generous. Hamburger chains like McDonalds could not operate without this arrangement of subsidized cattle growing.

In the face of the shortage of American cowboys like those in the billboard signs, the cattle ranchers in desperation took to importing Mexican *vaqueros* to ride the range. They had tried four-wheeled jeeps and even helicopters to cover the miles of open cattle range year-round. Gradually, the practice of importing cheap labor changed life in Wyoming, just as the introduction of African slavery changed American life thereafter. The *vaqueros* were housed out of town, with everything provided for them there, including women for entertainment. Only Mexican *vaqueros* were willing to ride for miles sometimes alone, even in winter, to watch over the thousands of cattle.

In time, Mexicans moved into the towns and set up housekeeping. While some *vaqueros* managed to bring up their wives and children from Mexico, others formed new families with American women. Sometimes these were second families. Local officials looked the other way at the breaking of immigration laws by pillars of the community because ranchers and the local economy depended on the Mexicans. At one meeting in a Catholic church social hall, I learned that local Chicanos had to argue hard with the priest to allow a civic meeting in the church location. The priest was from Italy and was not in tune with the Mexican-American community, despite its being the majority in his parish. A congressional candidate appeared and was hard at work shaking every hand he could. A local fellow explained that in his previous election the member of Congress had won by only a few hundred votes. In this crowd there were enough votes to decide his next campaign. Since the sparse population of Wyoming merits only one member of Congress, but two national senators, a modest increase of Mexican-American voters could gain major national importance. They would have to live through the beastly hot summers and the frigid winters, as well as the wind.

Local schools needed the advice I could give on how to help young Mexican children learn in American schools. Similar changes on farms and orchards in Washington, Oregon, and as far away as Michigan were taking place, changing local communities for the same reasons. Mexicans were gradually becoming part of the local scene. Even where housing segregation was practiced, young people met in school and intermarriage resulted. In many communities after Mexican immigrants became Americans, up to 33 percent of Mexican Americans were marrying people out of their group.

I learned during these lecture visits that relations with undocumented Mexican workers changed when their number grew beyond the local labor needs. Relations changed even more when Mexicans decided to settle down after harvest time rather than move on. At that point, local people started to refer to a "Mexican problem." Teachers sympathetic to the Mexican children would tell me about this attitudinal change among local leaders. Even after some resistance to undocumented workers emerged, selfish economic motives overcame prejudice. Meanwhile, during the standoff of opposing interests, countless communities were changing for good. Civic leaders that opposed undocumented immigration publicly were happy to profit from it privately. They were not the best role models.

Fred Ross became my role model in civic life. He was the organizer and long-range thinker for the Community Service Organization in East Los Angeles. Fred placed emphasis on developing community-based institutions rather than promoting events. "Institutions will carry on after us," he would say.

In Fred Ross's footsteps, I was the early mover for the founding of the California Association of Mexican-American School Board Members. With the financial help of the California School Board Members Association, to which we all belonged, a group of us persuaded the CSBA to schedule special sessions for the Mexican-American group. We paid for speakers that coached the group on politics, curriculum, and how to deal effectively with administrators. I recall surprising my school board colleagues by suggesting that they simply pass board motions to obtain a personal secretary and services like a car in order to become more effective. School superintendents would resist such things, but I reminded my *compañeros* that they employed the superintendent and were his or her bosses. The effectiveness of California Mexican-American school board members increased as a result of comparing notes and getting special help from paid insiders. The California delegation to the National School Board Members Association accomplished the same things at the national level. We formed a national group to monitor Mexican-American educational conditions and gain advice from experts. It was a surprise to learn that in the 1970s Mexican-American-elected school board members already numbered over a thousand, mostly in the Southwest. It's hard to measure the effect of these new organizational measures, but I am sure they were all to the good.

Chapter 18

Bilingual Education Comes to Los Angeles Schools

A major change took place in Los Angeles schools when the board elected Bill Johnston as the new superintendent. I was board president at the time and was able to steer the selection toward Johnston over more senior administrators. Bill and I became good friends and partners in numerous efforts to improve education in Los Angeles. Bill and I never lost sight of the fact that whatever happened in the Los Angeles schools was watched closely across the country.

The school board put into place new rules that made it easier to appoint minority administrators (one of the ninety-two walkout demands). When I joined the school board, there were only two Mexican-American high school and five elementary school principals. Before long, the number increased to seventy-five at all levels, and kept growing. The school board sought only the best administrators, but after we put affirmative action into practice, we defined this as an effort to meet the special needs of school communities. Sometimes a particular school needed a principal with certain racial or ethnic background for better communication between the school and the community. In short, the liberal school board now claimed that every administrator could not do a good job everywhere. Our care in applying this flexibility was rewarded by the success of the Mexican-American and black administrators who probably would not have been assigned by the traditional assessments that were very mathematical, measuring personal qualifications down to less than 1 percent out of a hundred points.

In 1967, President Lyndon B. Johnson signed the Bilingual Education Act. It carried out the essential arguments advanced by the president's old friend, Professor George I. Sánchez. It was my pleasure to be among the earliest supporters of this idea. From my platform on the Los Angeles School Board, I had the opportunity to speak in many places in support of bilingual education. Soon after the Bilingual Education Act went into effect, millions of dollars were handed out by the federal government to school districts for bilingual education programs.

Many fair-minded people had serious doubts about bilingual education. I convinced one of the most conservative board members to accept federal funds and support it by using arguments he understood. J.C. Chambers was a very intelligent man as well as very conservative politically. I once said, "J.C., you are an engineer and scientifically oriented. You know that at birth, talent is distributed at random. How would you have done in school if your teacher spoke in Chinese? Would you not have fallen behind until you learned Chinese? Let's say your parents spoke only English at home and could not help you learn Chinese. Would you not become discouraged, alienated, and maybe even delinquent? How many Einsteins or Picassos have we lost?" He agreed with this argument, and so the entire board agreed to accept federal funds for bilingual education.

At that time, the children in Los Angeles who needed this help were almost all Mexican American, so this program became a Mexican-American crusade like civil rights had become for blacks. From the start, bilingual education embodied some problems and created new ones. I believed then that bilingual education should be transitional. That is, children should be moved into English instruction as soon as possible. In view of the new jobs and school materials that came with federal dollars, some school districts kept children in bilingual classes much longer than necessary. Also, more and more Mexican-American educators saw this program as a jobs program. Compounding the new problems, some school districts diverted federal bilingual aid for other educational purposes. This diversion of funds made bilingual education appear to cost more than it really did.

Much good came from bilingual education, but opposition against it grew. Many school districts hired teachers that were not fully bilingual or had little training to teach in bilingual classrooms. University schools of education were slow to train teachers. Actually, most universities did not know how to train bilingual teachers. Original opponents of the idea were joined by those who opposed what looked like favoritism to Mexican Americans. As immigration from across the seas increased, bilingual education faced the challenge of helping Chinese, Russian, Vietnamese, Korean, and other students. These new demands increased opposition to bilingual education. Anti-immigrant feelings added to the educational problem, making it a political issue. In some cities that were ports of entry, more and more Americans believed that they were losing their country to the immigrants, especially the Spanish-speaking ones.

The social and economic issues, as well as simple racism, complicated the evaluation of bilingual education. The growing flood of poor, undocumented workers from Mexico was the last straw for opponents of bilingual education. Nativists in growing numbers demanded "English-only" education. Others demanded English-only communication between employees. Some public opinion polls showed that even the parents of immigrants wanted English-only instruction. The form of the questions asked in some surveys helped shape the answers, and so the results were faulty.

A basic question lies at the bottom of the argument over bilingual education. How can we define an American? Is it language, religion, culture, race, residency, or allegiance that defines an American? The question is still part of an American dilemma. As usual in public life, both sides are partly right and partly wrong. For our part, Pat and I taught the children Spanish as well as English at home. Actually, they should have learned French, too. Children in Europe learn several languages in childhood. After the European Union was formed, all twelve countries began to require that all children learn two other languages in public school as a matter of course. Doesn't this make fun of our concern that children learn only in English?

Our school board meetings were broadcast live on television because some of them were more than just lively. At one board meeting, J.C. Chambers was red with rage and stomped over with clenched fists as if to punch me. I just sat there and removed my glasses. After a minute, which seemed longer, he stormed off in silence. Oddly enough, J.C. and I became good friends in time, even though we often disagreed. He was very intelligent, and I never forgot that he cared for kids as much as I did.

The television age came to our district during my service. We opened a separate channel available to the public. This cost several million dollars. In order to have a first-class TV channel, we hired one of the best commercial managers to launch it. In time, other districts across the country set up their own TV stations, but most were closed circuit—that is, they worked only within the district. Our TV channel was soon offering educational and cultural programs available to the general public, many of which were telecast nationally. In later years, the quality of programming declined due to shortage of funds and weak management, but at least the instrument was operating.

School Superintendent Bill Johnston had a very good friend who was a Catholic priest in Pacoima, a Mexican-American barrio in the San Fernando Valley. Father Luis Balbuena was born in Spain, was very Castillian in his manners, and spoke a Spanish that was a pleasure to hear. As the issue of how to help immigrant children grew more intense, Father Balbuena concluded that dominant Spanish-speaking children should be taught basic subjects in Spanish while they learned English as quickly as possible. Father Balbuena kept track of politics and knew about my proposals for some form of bilingual education since the time of my election campaign. The superintendent, who was Catholic, spoke with Father Balbuena, and, before long, a pilot bilingual program was opened in the Santa Rosa Parish School for public school pupils after school. That's how bilingual education started in Los Angeles. Other school districts looked over our shoulders as the results seemed to be good. When the school board formally established bilingual education with federal funds, we intended that it be a transitional form of assistance. As soon as the children learned enough English, they should move into regular English classes. With so many children speaking other foreign languages, we could not serve them all. Spanish was about 90 percent of the need, however.

The Chicano movement across the nation grew stronger all the time during the 1970s. Some within it believed that Spanish-language instruction should be maintained even after children could learn in English. I disagreed with this "maintenance" approach on two grounds. English should receive emphasis in public education because the students were Americans, to begin with, or would be growing up in an English-speaking world, in any case. I also predicted growing opposition to bilingual education, should it appear to divide students into two groups, both using public funds. I believed that, should parents want to maintain the second language, this could be done at home. My view on this was influenced in great part by my childhood experiences. The Japanese and Jewish families in our barrio had not demanded bilingual education but maintained their language by activities at home and as part of their cultural and religious life.

Politics and public education cannot be separated. An example of this was the effort by some black Americans in Los Angeles to obtain federal War on Poverty funds to establish a bilingual program for ghetto English. Ghetto English, supposedly, was the way that low-income black people spoke among themselves, using slang and new words made up of old ones. In view of the nationwide turmoil over civil rights and extensive white support for black Americans, this demand required careful handling. After considerable discussion and emotional public statements on both sides, the board rejected the black community's request. We stated that ghetto English was a dialect of English, not a language that could be considered part of a bilingual curriculum.

I gained the resentment of many black leaders because I was very clear in opposing support for ghetto English. For champions of ghetto English, I was the personification of Spanish-speaking folks who were gaining nationwide benefit of millions of dollars for bilingual education. Some black leaders wanted some of that money. I failed to persuade black educator friends of my point of view. At the same time, I lost Chicano friends who resented my support for transitional rather than maintenance Spanish/English bilingual education.

The news of the assassination of Reverend Martin Luther

King reached the board while it was in session. Reverend James Jones cried out, "My lord, you have killed him." While he was on the school board, Reverend Jones and I agreed on most things, but he was not quite the same again after the loss of Reverend King. Some bitterness was evident in his struggle for better education for black children. Reverend Jones retired, and Diane Watson, a black former teacher, was elected. She and I clashed over many things and became political opponents. And, in time, she got even with me.

Our family solution to the bilingual education controversy was to break the piggy bank so that all of us could travel throughout Mexico one summer and on another occasion throughout Spain. In addition, Carmen and Katie went to study one year at the University of Salamanca, in the heart of Castille, where Spanish originated and where it was still most pure. Now and then, Pat and I recall how we waited for their Iberia Airlines 747 to roar down the runway at LAX. We cried quietly as our little girls went off on their own. They had a wonderful time, of course, and returned with an ability to speak good Spanish, which did not get in the way of graduating summa cum laude in English from college.

Chapter 19

The School Integration Issue in Los Angeles

Integration of schools was probably the biggest education crisis while I served on the school board. This issue sharply divided the citizens of Los Angeles and the nation as well. For several years I promoted voluntary methods to implement the integration of black and Hispanic students with the majority of white students. Mexican-American students made up almost all of the Spanish-surnamed in the school district. In time, their percentage of the total Spanish-surnamed dropped as Central Americans from Nicaragua, El Salvador, and Guatemala streamed in due to civil wars at home. In the 1970s, all Spanish-surnamed students were only about 25 percent of the district's students. By the 1990s their numbers had increased to over 60 percent and continued to rise.

The integration crisis in Los Angeles schools was provoked by a court order to completely integrate the district in a fashion approved by a judge who had control over the issue. Ironically, this court order was issued when the School Community Advisory Councils (CACs) had just started to give parents considerable voice in their children's schools. The CACs were not intended to establish integration. They were a means to give "power to the people," as a slogan put it in those days. Overwhelmingly, Hispanic parents cared little for integration and instead wanted quality education in their local schools. I agreed with these folks and with the black parents and others who felt the same way. With rare exceptions, blacks in Los Angeles felt pressured to support integration championed by national black leadership and liberal whites. Now that the courts across the nation were requiring integration, to oppose it was to appear on the side of white racists. The fact was that those opposing integration were not all racists, but emotions regarding integration were stronger than reason.

School board meetings saw debates that provoked near riots in the packed audience. All of this was telecast so that board members and especially speakers played to the cameras. I could not stop being a professor, and so I tried to be clear and objective. This did not always work well. I recall that board member Diane Watson had a very special manner for expressing herself. She was vehement about racism, and her solution for it was to mix all the children, no matter what. She would speak at length with great emotion when she got the floor, rambling on and on as she sought to make a point in the course of her long talk. On one occasion I earned her eternal hostility. After one of her long monologues, I asked, "Miss Watson, just what did you want to say?" Everyone else just smiled as the board went on as if she had not said anything. If Diane's looks could kill, I would have dropped dead.

At this time Los Angeles schools were segregated. Since students attended schools near where they lived, and housing itself was largely segregated, white, Hispanic, black, and Asian pupils were concentrated in their local schools. Each group sometimes made up 80 to 95 percent of the student body at a given school. When these conditions exist due to residential patterns, this segregation is called "de facto," or a product of actual conditions. When races are separated by official action, this is called "de jure" segregation. Los Angeles schools were segregated de facto.

Los Angeles' Chinatown and Little Tokyo communities were the result of historical racism that made it hard for Chinese or Japanese Americans to live outside their own neighborhoods. Tourists from other areas of town occasionally visited these colorful cultural centers but resisted Asian families moving into their neighborhoods. Much the same was true with Mexican barrios and black ghettos. I recall people coming to our barrio for Mexican food and to Watts to hear good jazz along south Central Boulevard. These tourists would not live in these neighborhoods nor would they want the people there to move into their neighborhoods.

Los Angeles schools had no "de jure" segregation because the district did not enforce racial separation. In fact, the school district offered free transportation to any minority family that wanted to transfer its children out of a barrio or a ghetto school. This transfer policy cost a lot of money. The court claimed that our open enrollment policy was insufficient to eliminate segregation. That was certainly true.

The subject of school integration merits a more detailed book. I always opposed legally enforced segregation and, for that matter, legally enforced integration also. Maybe a moderate point of view reflects mixed feelings—mine surely were mixed. There was no simple solution to this historical problem, and I leaned toward moderate and voluntary solutions at a time when feelings on all sides were so intense. As in other cases, I was in the worst place to be: the middle.

For the first time, minority parents were having a greater impact on their local schools by means of the Community Advisory Committees. Other measures like affirmative action, more minority administrators and teachers, better textbooks, and a curriculum that began to tell the story of minority group contributions to American history were having a good effect. Such educational reforms expanded opportunities for all students while being acceptable to the majority of white voters. My support for voluntary measures stemmed from the conviction that if the majority population became hostile to public schools due to enforced integration, only bad things for public schools would come about.

Professor Raymond McHugh and I codirected the first national summer Institute on the Role and Contribution of Minority Groups to U.S. History in 1965. The National Defense Education Act funded the institute for another two summers, after which the staff simply burned out due to the work. We selected department chairs and senior teachers from applicants scattered all over the country. They were coming for a high-powered summer course to increase their ability to train other teachers across the country. By the time we threw in the towel, several hundred professionals were scattered from coast to coast, prepared to improve public school teaching in this vital area that addressed prejudice based on ignorance. During the course of the first summer institute, the famous Watts Riots broke out in Los Angeles, as if to prove the need for such progressive education. We had seen the handwriting on the wall accurately, it seems; however, no other such programs for teachers were in operation for years after we stopped ours.

In the early 1970s, Spanish-surnamed students were slightly more than 25 percent of district enrollment, but barrio schools were almost all Spanish surnamed. I use Spanish surname because this term included children from all the Spanish-speaking countries of Latin America. In order to provide a numerical proportionate balance, as the mandatory integrationists wanted in every school, more than half of the Spanish-surnamed students from barrio schools would have to be transferred to other schools. This would make room for whites, Asians, and black students who would take their place in the barrio schools. The transferred students would be scattered all over the city. Their bus ride meant getting up about five in the morning and, in many cases, spending two to three hours on a bus every day. The incoming students to the barrio schools would have to undergo the same inconveniences.

The school district would have to buy more buses than could be produced in time, so several private bus companies stood to gain profitable contracts for moving a small army of students in opposite directions daily. Hispanic parents resisted all of this, as did Asian families and most whites. Community Advisory Committees would be handicapped. Poor minority parents and community folks would find it hard to travel across town in the evening to the schools where their children were now attending. White parents were reluctant to enter the barrio or ghetto to visit their children's schools in the evening. Although this experience would be good for them, they resisted having to do it.

One of the years that I was board president, I was able to shape a voluntary integration program, which the board approved but the judge turned down. Board member Professor Robert Doctor believed that voluntary measures could not be extensive enough nor get court approval, but he had been a friend and colleague at CSUN, and together, we shaped a plan anyway. District staff polished the idea, gave it a better name, and the district offered it to the judge. The majority of the board crossed our fingers, but we needed more fingers than we had.

The essence of our plan for voluntary integration was the establishment of numerous new schools where students of all races would be encouraged to attend because of the school's outstanding special programs. Bob and I called these "Concentrated Learning Centers," and the district staff changed the name to "Magnet Schools." At each magnet school, the highest quality educational experience in music, art, science, or some other subject area would be offered by special staff. The district would make these schools attractive, and it would be an honor to attend them. Attendance would be voluntary, but in each magnet school the district would preserve ethnic and racial percentages that were acceptable to the judge. We hoped this special instruction would spill over to the regular schools. All the student numbers and busing plans were figured out. Nevertheless, the judge turned down this last effort at volunteer busing because it was not sufficient to affect the entire district. It wasn't sufficient for complete integration, but the public would have accepted it.

The Judge ordered mandatory busing across the whole district on a simple mathematical basis. In the middle of all this, a proposal before the state legislature proposed that the Los Angeles Unified School District be split up in order to resolve segregation. It is interesting that a white state senator opposing integration and a black state senator supporting integration agreed to sponsor such a law. The inspiration for this cooperation between opposites was that blacks and whites would have their own district, thus going their own separate ways. Integration would no longer be an issue, but Spanish-surnamed students would be split up into one of the two new and independent school districts. This was a black/white apartheid solution that ignored the Spanish-surnamed and Asians.

During a public debate on the Harmer-Green Bill, as it was called, I was almost assaulted in a public debate by black State Senator Billy Green. He stood way over me, large as a football running back. I really think my argument against dividing the city into black, white, brown, and yellow school districts made him so mad that he walked over and, with clenched fists, put his nose so close to mine I could feel him exhaling like a bull in the arena. I just stared back at him and said nothing because I didn't stand a chance of defending myself in a civil manner. All I knew about hand-to-hand combat I had learned in the military, and if my instincts came into play, I would fight to defend myself with different rules. The TV cameras discouraged him from doing what he wanted to do. This project to divide the district went down in failure.

A peaceful social war ensued as the Los Angeles Unified School District moved quickly to implement the mandatory court order to integrate fully. If the board had not obeyed the judge, he had the power to take over the administration of the district and do the job with new officers. This sort of thing had happened elsewhere in the country, and in every case it was a terrible mess. The board traveled to some of these districts and saw the outcome of a court takeover, so we did what we preferred not to do.

My good friend Doctor, who championed mandatory integration along with Diane Watson, lost his post in the next elections. A political group called "Bus Stop" became a major political force in the city due to its opposition to busing. Antibusing board members gained a majority on the school board, but they had no choice but to obey the court order. I was not enjoying service on the school board anymore.

Many thousands of white school children were taken out of public schools by parents who opposed busing into minority schools or accepting minority students into their local schools. This "white flight" had been predicted, but the judge paid no attention to the possibility because it had no bearing on the actual legal issue. Legally, he was correct, but socially and educationally, he was wrong. Private schools sprang up like mushrooms to handle the new business. It cost these parents dearly to send children to these private schools while they continued to pay taxes for public schools.

As the district became predominately minority, I noted a loss of support for it in the state legislature and the general public. As I started to write this book, my son was teaching at James Monroe High School in the heart of the San Fernando Valley. It used to be a white high school with a modest number of minority students. Thanks to integration, dozens of huge yellow buses brought in black and Hispanic youngsters to make up the majority of the students. After school, you could see a long procession of buses belching black exhaust as they got on to the freeway headed for the inner city, where the minority students lived. Numerous yellow bus caravans snaked their way on freeways across the metropolitan area daily in different directions.

As a historian, I pondered the discrimination that had brought us to this pivotal point in our history. Like a mental illness early in our history, racism had brought some Americans to believe they were superior and more American than more recent arrivals. This idea is called "nativism" by historians. It arose almost two hundred years ago as immigrants from Europe arrived and mixed with the English-speaking people who had come earlier. The new Americans spoke other languages and practiced religions that were not Protestant. Resistance to the second wave of newcomers from Scandinavia, Germany, Ireland, and so forth produced the idea that the newcomers were not really American. They were not only different but bad. Violence against foreigners from Europe was common before the Civil War. Sometimes, English-speaking Protestants burned down the churches of the newcomers. Early in the twentieth century, immigrants from southern Europe added to the mix, and there arose increased hostility to immigrants, even though the newcomers were becoming Americans as fast as they could. My family history was different in some ways. Due to the First World

War and the labor shortage it had created, Mexicans were welcomed until the Great Depression of the 1930s. Mexican refugees of the Mexican Revolution just crossed the border on foot to jobs waiting for them to fill.

When we add white hostility to Indians and the practice of African slavery, anti-immigrant feelings had found fertile soil among many people. Although much of this hostility has lessened, most of it has survived. How often do we see a movie in which an Indian is the "good guy"? I can still recall the election of John F. Kennedy to the presidency in 1960. It made history because he embodied two elements of prejudice. He was not only Irish, but Roman Catholic as well.

Americans with an Hispanic heritage occupy a unique place in the controversy as to who is an American. To begin with, Hispanic colonists were in the American Southwest and Florida centuries before English settlers colonized the Northeast. However, the violence connected with the territorial expansion of the United States brought Mexican Americans into a social status in which they were regarded as only slightly better than Indians. This prejudice was very much alive when I was elected to the school board two centuries after U.S. independence.

Mindful of the need to change impressions about us, I always tried to set an example of a Mexican American who could conduct public business for everyone. I am not sure I was successful.

Chapt

CHICANO STUDIES IN AMERICAN HIGHER EDUCATION

California State University, Northridge was growing rapidly during the 1960s, so our department of history decided to hire another professor at the rank of assistant professor. There was much turmoil on the campus during this time. Students of all colors were protesting against the war in Vietnam, discrimination in jobs, educational segregation, and so forth. Adding to the confusion, the trustees had just appointed a new president.

As a member of the department selection committee, I suggested Dr. Rudy Acuña for the new position. I knew he would make an excellent addition to the department. As a local Mexican American who taught at Pierce Community College, he knew the community and was a very good teacher. I was the only Mexican-American professor in a department of twenty, so it seemed like a good idea to have another in a community like ours, where the Spanish-surnamed population was passing 25 percent.

The committee turned down Rudy's application in favor of a well-qualified white person from out of state. What turned the vote against Rudy was a remark to the selection committee by its chairman. After I presented the arguments for Rudy, he said to the committee in a fatherly manner, "Julian, we already have one of your people." The committee majority voted with the chairman, and Rudy stayed at Pierce.

Shortly after this, our university underwent a terrible riot in which police clubbed and arrested hundreds of students. The students were protesting against the Vietnam War with its growing casualties. This was the first war in which the American public could see live battle action on television—not the acting in movies, but real young people getting killed. All of a sudden, war was not glamorous. The entire nation was shocked by this. Later on during the American invasion of Grenada and Panama, as well as the Gulf War against Iraq, our government kept TV cameramen and reporters under control. The public saw on TV only what our government wanted the public to see. It is, therefore, no surprise that these conflicts were popular. The government saw to it that antiwar protests like those at our university were avoided.

Our university had just gained a new president from the Midwest, where such student actions were rare. President James Cleary had not yet arrived on the campus, and our acting president was in a jam. One group of students had seized the administration building and would not let anyone leave for a period of time. What I believe provoked the kidnapping of the building was that the Los Angeles police were swarming all over the campus, with helicopters in the air and tear gas on the ground. I am convinced it was a mistake to call in the police because they tend to demonstrate their authority. Antiwar protesters were a good target for the police since they were often regarded as unpatriotic. Some foolish students threw rocks at the police, and the riot began. Police clubs flashed up and down as students scattered. To see all of this was frightening, and tragic.

President Cleary may have been sorry he took the job. The lack of minority students and professors was one of the reasons for the protests, so Cleary appointed committees to recommend solutions to these problems. One committee comprised of professors recruited black and Mexican-American students practically off the streets. Special (that is, lower) entrance requirements opened the doors to marginal students, but lowered the temperature among the youthful protesters.

The president sought to calm down the passions and resolve many problems by giving in to minority student demands to establish Black Studies and Chicano Studies departments. These would have equal standing with other traditional departments. They could hire professors, create courses, and carry on all the usual activities on a basis of equality. The traditional departments opposed this measure as giving in to minority pressure. Most of the other professors could not understand how such departments could fit into the traditional framework of university departments.

The Mexican-American students demanded a separate department to study all aspects of their lives and their people's role in American history. The Chicano Studies department would be interdisciplinary by teaching several subjects, including all aspects of Chicano history. Cleary was anxious to calm down campus life, so he agreed to this and told opposing faculty to accept these changes. We were now called "Strife-torn Valley State" across the country. Cleary wanted to erase that harmful impression by restoring normal life.

The committee for nominating a founding chairman for Chicano Studies reviewed candidates from all over the country. Rudy's name stood out. The committee proposed that he be made founding chairman of Chicano Studies at the rank of full professor. Cleary may have swallowed hard but agreed. This is the highest rank among professors, and usually, it takes many years to gain that rank. I had just become full professor after about eight years at the university. I felt vindicated after my department's rejection of Rudy as an assistant professor, and I was delighted for him, the campus, and the community. Rudy and I had worked on some community educational projects before, and this gave me confidence he would be a powerful force in higher education. It certainly turned out that way.

A year before I ran for the school board, Rudy and I decided that we would write textbooks for public schools that portrayed the role and contributions of Mexican Americans in national history. I picked elementary and middle grades. Rudy took high school and college. We conferred at length regularly. He taught me how to write at the reading level of the students in grade schools. This took some practice because I was trained for language and concepts at the college level.

What a coincidence! At the time of the 1968 walkouts, my first book appeared in print. It was *Mexican Americans: Past, Present and Future.* It was the first such book in American history in two respects: first of all, its subject matter and, second, it appeared in separate English and Spanish editions. These books were written for secondary schools. Immediately afterward, I edited an anthology of original historical sources that fit in with the textbook. The anthology, *The Mexican American in American History,* was equally suitable for a college edition, which appeared as *Viva La Raza.* In this manner, students could read actual accounts that enriched what the textbook related. Other books followed.

I stopped writing traditional scholarly articles and decided to write for younger people in view of the greater need. Later on, I coauthored *California: Five Centuries of Cultural Contrast* for colleges. This was fun compared to public school texts. This diversion changed my academic life from research to writing about things that were immediately influential.

Rudy's first book for high school was also the first of its kind. His second book caused quite a fuss because he called it *Occupied America.* He was as harsh on white settlers of the Southwest as they deserved. Many pioneers traveling westward said, "The only good Indian is a dead one," and many acted the same way toward Mexican Americans. After 1848, when the United States seized the Southwest from Mexico, Mexican Americans became an oppressed minority in their own lands. He was very accurate, and so his book distressed many people who liked to know only nice things about the past. Chicano Studies began rewriting American history by telling it more fully.

My books went out of print in a few years, even as the need for them grew. The publisher of my books was bought by a giant weapons producing firm. American Book Company now belonged to Litton Industries. The new owners of American Book Company were not in tune with the world of publishing. Like many other highly profitable firms, Litton avoided paying federal income taxes by spending some of its profits buying a company that had no bearing on its main line of business: weapons design and building.

Traditional book publishers knew that some books can shape public thinking, even though the books don't sell in massive numbers. Litton cared less for the social impact of a book than it did for how much money it brought in to help pay for the purchase. Many hundreds of American Book Company books were dropped from publication in favor of popular books that scored on the best-seller lists. Since American Book Company owned the copyright for my books, only they could publish them. I could do nothing, and the books disappeared as soon as the existing copies ran out, although the need for them was increasing.

The future got even with Litton Industries. When the war in Vietnam ended and orders for weapons dropped, Litton suffered hard times. Litton sold American Book Company to raise the cash it needed, and then the buyers sold the company again. The original publishing company that had showed courage by printing much-needed books just ceased to exist. Schools wanted the books but could not buy them. Some teachers have written for my permission to make photocopies.

Another failure awaited me. A set of my textbooks died when Aardvark Books went out of business. I had edited an eight-volume series of readers for elementary school, starting with first grade. The eight volumes in English were accompanied by a Spanish-language series. Each of these books was filled with pleasant stories about growing up. I wrote one book, but the others were stories written by various teachers and even some children. One of the most interesting books was for grade six. *Traditions in the Barrio* tells about customs that are strong forces in shaping young Mexican Americans as they grow up: customs like respect for parents, family loyalty, taking care of younger siblings, love for your cousins, and so forth.

I wrote my books for everyone—that is, they related to Mexican-American history and life, but they tried to make these topics interesting for everyone. This attitude came from my personal experience as a child in the barrio. In addition, our extended family is a United Nations because we are not all Mexican in background. We have a Jew, a German, an Englishman, a black, and an Italian among us. My brothers and sisters, as well as their children, have married outside of the Mexican family. This variety is evident at Christmas, when we all get together. The extended Nava family is like many other Mexican-American families. It occurs to me that we may look like what everyone else will look like in the future, if intermarriage overcomes traditional discrimination.

The books I wrote while I was on the school board were my major contribution to the Chicano Movement. More people may have read them than the numbers of those who were personally affected by my service on the school board. Before long, younger authors wrote better books about Mexican Americans, their roles and contributions to American history. It has been nice to see the baton passed on to others.

I decided not to run for reelection to the school board after three terms. Twelve years were enough. When I look back, I wonder how I got involved in so many projects and got so many things done. I think that when 1979 came around, I was ready to end this school board experience, as well as the intense political life that it had involved. The controversy over integration had become so intense that we unlisted our telephone number. On some occasions, I wore a flack jacket at the recommendation of the police. It was heavy and made me look fat. After twelve years, I figured that it was someone else's turn to go through all this.

What clinched our decision was the ballot measure that changed the way to elect school board members. Now, each member was to be elected from a seventh part of the entire district, like city council people. This single-member district system seemed more democratic than at-large elections, in which each school board member was elected from the entire district. Minority groups fought hard to gain the single-member ballot measure. Both Hispanics and blacks hoped to get more than one school board member elected. I opposed the single-member plan and lost many supporters among Chicano political activists for this. As it turned out, only one black and one Chicano were elected to the board after me for a long time.

Opponents to my position became annoyed when I would say, "I told you so." Spanish-surnamed students were scattering to live throughout the huge metropolitan area, and so most would be a minority in most of the new districts. With elections at large, every board member had to pay attention to us because we were a factor in their election. This was no longer to be true. The coalition of various minority groups and white liberals dissolved to some extent because now each group sought its own interests. Under the previous system, each board member affected the entire school district, and this was a force for unity of purpose. Every group had to be concerned about each board member because each of these individuals affected local schools. In turn, each board member had to care for all children because all voting parents in the district elected each board member. I could not be a board member for only Mexican Americans in this system of at-large elections. Now each racial or ethnic group was going to be on its own. I did not like the new system, so this also contributed to my decision to retire from the school board in 1979.

Me as a young boy.

U.S. naval combat aircrewman, 1945.

Pat and I on our wedding day, June 30, 1962.

President of the school board in Los Angeles, California.

My arrival to present ambassadors' credentials in Mexico.

My family and I as I receive the command for ambassadorship to Mexico from President Jimmy Carter.

The Nava family during Julian's campaign for mayor of Los Angeles.

Nava on the campaign trail.

Me as pallbearer for César Chávez, 1993.

César Chávez's funeral in 1993.

A *charreada* in Zacatecas.

At the ruins of my great-grandmother's home in Tepetongo, Mexico.

Chapter 21

Our *Charro* Traditions

I should never have agreed to buy the beautiful Shetland pony we called Half Pint. She pulled a red cart, and everyone except me thought it was a great idea. This started the horse period in my family's life. Before long we had four horses, saddles, a trailer, tack that filled the garage, and constant battles with flies, not to mention collecting the manure. Luckily, the backyard was ample for stalls and an exercise arena. Our home was on the edge of housing in the San Fernando Valley, so we could saddle up and ride just a block away. In time, new housing cut us off, so we acquired a four-horse trailer and went elsewhere to ride.

The horse I acquired, Canelo, was trained for Mexican *charro* competitions. A *charro* is a Mexican rider who has a highly trained horse and competes in *charreadas* (a type of rodeo). The owner had trained Canelo since youth and enjoyed riding him for numerous years of competition up and down the state. Canelo was about fifteen years old and was well known among *charros* in southern California. The owner sold him because he wanted a younger horse for competition. These fellows knew horses and related to them as if they were people. Canelo could compete in all nine events in Mexican competition and knew far more about riding than I did. Now and then he would look around at me as if to say, "What's the matter with you?" In spite of all his energy and skill, he was completely obedient and gentle. He was *de buena ley* (obedient), as Mexicans say.

We joined a group of *charros* who undertook to build a *lienzo* or arena near our home. Usually, these guys dress in fine riding clothes, whose Mexican characteristics go back three centuries. *Charros* are not *vaqueros,* which translates literally into cowboys. *Vaqueros* simply work with cattle. Although some *charros* do *vaquero* work, most try to act like gentlemen riders. Their horses are especially beautiful. My *charro* outfit cost about $300 at that time due to the silver ornaments on the jacket and trousers. The Association of Charros's Emiliano Zapata got a permit to build an arena with stalls and parking in Hansen Dam. It took all the politicking I could muster as a school board member to persuade city officials to give us the permit. The resistance to our permit came down to prejudice against Mexican-style riding. It is true that in *charreadas,* cattle and horses are sometimes hurt (without mentioning the horsemen). However, only *charreadas* were banned in Los Angeles, although cowboy rodeos produced injuries to the animals as well.

Over many weekends, entire families contributed to building the stadium and network of corrals. The men worked with tractors and hand tools, while women and children cheered us on. During Mexican meals prepared by the women, there was always someone to play a guitar. The rest of the time, pickup doors were opened wide and *norteñas*—Mexican songs—blared out. It's handy to know how to work with your hands, and I must confess my respect for a man drops a bit when he can't fix something. Among the *charros,* we had every skill needed to do the enormous job.

Carmen and Katie practiced for hours with other youths

to perform Mexican folk dances at *charreadas.* In time, huge crowds came to see *charro* competitions that lasted all day Sunday.

In the American Southwest today, there are more *charros* and *charreadas* than in Mexico because of immigration. It's part of the desire of immigrants to keep alive traditions that make them feel at home. Strict rules govern everything about *charreadas,* and champions are known everywhere among Mexican horsemen. Beto Cueva, our close friend, was *un charro completo*—that is, he had a national championship in each of the nine events. Every Mexican horseman I ever met knew about Beto and spoke of him with reverence, even though Beto was simply a night watchman at a movie studio.

While we were living in Mexico City, the Los Angeles city officials ordered the *lienzo* shut down. Our friends dismantled the entire installation and returned it to its natural conditions. We had aspired to building a cultural center connected with Mexican horsemanship but lost a chance to do something significant in the City of Angels, which our ancestors founded. I just shook my head upon hearing about this reversal and remembered that discrimination against Mexican Americans in Los Angeles was still vigorous.

Indeed, as Mexican Americans made some progress, discrimination seemed to increase in order to keep us in a subordinate place. Even African Americans, who had gained some political power, worked against us in order to control the modest concessions made to minority groups. The site for the *lienzo* was taken over by a white fellow, who proceeded to build a giant cowboy riding center. Today, only some large sycamore trees mark the location of our beautiful failure.

Chapter 22

Black and Brown Conflict over a University Presidency

Two opportunities to be a president of a California state university opened up as I was leaving the school board, and I lost out on both. The first, at California State Polytechnic University-Pomona, was my fault. The state university system chancellor told me privately that he could swing the trustees to my selection if I applied for the presidency. Pat and I worried about the bad smog conditions in the Pomona Valley and its effect on the children's health, so I declined the offer. I applied instead for the presidency at California State University-Los Angeles, close to where I grew up and in the middle of the largest Mexican-American community in the nation. The smog there was no better, but there were compensations. The loss of this post was not my fault.

Cal State L.A. was surrounded by a community of about 75 percent Hispanics, mostly Mexican Americans. However, only 20 percent of the university student body was Hispanic. Due to my school board experience, I knew the area well and especially the condition of the public schools that fed into the university. Knowledge of the community is important because each campus is required to serve the community in its service area.

Most presidential selections in California are political, frankly. When candidates are equally qualified in most respects, special considerations become the deciding factors. The head of the statewide university system was a friend, and while he recommended me, it was the trustees who actually made the selection. Even statewide-elected officials like the governor of California sometimes expressed a preference in the more important cases of university presidencies. This campus presidency was one of them because the enrollment at Cal State L.A. was more than 25,000, and it was the most important of four state universities in the Los Angeles region.

I made the rounds, talking to trustees and the governor, Jerry Brown, about how important it was to at last have a Mexican American as head of a major California public university. Up to 1979, not a single Mexican American had been appointed to a metropolitan campus in the system of nineteen universities. A friend, Tomás Arciniega, had just been appointed to a remote, new campus in Bakersfield as the first Mexican-American campus president in the statewide system. He was eminently qualified, and yet he was sent to a new campus in the middle of a farming region, where most Mexican Americans were poor farmworkers and suffered discrimination. Since he was an educational leader by national standards, he should have been appointed to a major metropolitan campus, I felt. President Arciniega agreed to withdraw his request to move from Bakersfield to Los Angeles in order to avoid both of us applying for the same position. Besides, since he was already a president helping me become one would make two Mexican-American university presidents in a statewide system.

By 1970, Mexican Americans and other Hispanics had accepted the common reference to themselves as "brown." The United States was drifting into a condition in which its population was divided into colors: whites, blacks, browns, reds, and yellows. Rivalries between black and brown leadership caused friction over the few openings made available by institutions that were dominated by the white majority. In such matters, one had to touch bases with representatives of the major ethnic, racial, and political groups in order to arrange a workable solution. It seemed logical that the social and educational conditions at this campus argued for my selection. The trustees had made two black presidential appointments already in California, although Mexican Americans outnumbered black Americans two to one in the state.

After making the rounds of confidential talks with white, black, and Jewish trustees, I gained the support of Governor Brown and the state superintendent of public instruction, Wilson Riles (a black American). It seemed clear that I could count on a majority of trustees to gain the appointment. However, when the vote was taken, everyone was surprised that I lost by an eight-to-seven vote in favor of a black educator from New Jersey. James Rosser could not tell a taco from a tamale, so to speak. He did not know the area or the politics at play. Chancellor Glenn Dumke and Governor Jerry Brown were surprised at the outcome and wondered about the statewide political consequences.

I lost the selection because one favorable vote failed to show up, as promised, and two supporters switched loyalty at the last minute. About a week later, I spoke to Dr. Claudia Hampton, a black trustee who had promised to vote for me. At the last minute she abstained, costing me one vital vote. I had known Claudia for the twelve years that I served on the school board. I thought we were good friends. Claudia was most embarrassed when I asked for an explanation of her abstention. She told me that a former school board member, State Senator Diane Watson, threatened her if she supported me over a black candidate. Blacks must stick together, Watson said, according to Hampton, and if a prominent black educational administrator like Claudia supported a Mexican American over one of her own, she would have to pay dearly for it. I guess Watson never forgot we had argued over integration while we were both on the school board. She had now found a way to get even with me.

The state superintendent of public instruction took another road. Rather than break his promise to vote for me by voting for another, Riles did not attend the meeting, even after he had said, "Julian, I owe you one." He was referring to the fact that I had been very instrumental in his election as the first black to statewide office. Both of us had been candidates in the statewide primary race for superintendent of public instruction against a very conservative incumbent, James Rafferty. I only got 17 percent of the votes statewide with a modestly financed campaign, but my votes deprived Rafferty of a majority in the primary election. Wilson was in the runoff with Rafferty, and with my warm endorsement won, with most Mexican Americans voting for him. In spite of numerous requests that I support Rafferty, who liked Hispanics as a matter of fact, I supported Riles for two reasons: He was a fellow minority member and I agreed with his ideas for education. This was in spite of the fact that after many campaign talks across the state, Riles had very little to say that addressed real problems. He expected folks to support him because he was a tall, good-looking black educator with a nice, sonorous voice. Among white folks, Rafferty had become unpopular because of his personal manner and the lower educational achievement in state schools.

I guess that although personal reasons varied somewhat, votes switched to the selection of a black for president at Cal State L.A. because black needs were seen as more important than Mexican-American needs. It seemed as though the fact that this campus was in the heart of the largest barrio in the nation was not as important as helping black Americans obtain leadership positions. Some black leaders across the nation were criticizing American Jews as economic oppressors in the ghettoes, and some even threatened violence against Jews. The Jewish member of the trustees also set aside her promise of support for me and voted for Rosser.

After this event, I was very selective in supporting black causes. My convictions about social justice did not change, but I came to realize firsthand that many black leaders were willing to step over other minorities in their quest for more opportunities. As word of the betrayal spread among Hispanics in the Southwest, many others did what I did. Black/brown coalitions pretty much evaporated. What Riles and Hampton did was no surprise in some respects. Affirmative action efforts since the War on Poverty Program began in the 1960s were intended to help all minorities, including women. However, white and black Americans pretty much ignored Hispanics until black needs were met. What happened to me confirmed sentiments among Hispanics across the country that they must struggle against blacks who behaved like gringos.

More bad things happened as I was retiring from the school board. In an effort to make amends, Chancellor Glen Dumke urged me to apply for the presidency of Fresno State University, a major campus in the heart of the agricultural San Joaquin Valley. This effort proved to be futile for other reasons. The long interview with the presidential selection committee went very well. The members were well acquainted with my years of teaching at home and abroad, my books, consulting everywhere, and long service on the school board. Some interviewers were aware of what had happened at Cal State L.A. How this affected them I could not be sure, but I believe it was damaging to my candidacy because their campus presidency looked like a consolation prize for me.

As it turned out, I was not a finalist to be interviewed by the trustees. I soon learned why. One of the interview committee members telephoned and declined to identify himself, although I recognized his voice. In short, he said I was one of the strongest candidates and should have been passed on to the trustees as a finalist. He reported that one committee member opposed me clearly by saying, "Anyone but Nava." My anonymous friend also reported, "Julian, you must take into account the community around California State University-Fresno. Folks here see Mexicans mostly as farmworkers, and not as their university president. You would not fit in. I'm sorry and ashamed of these folks, but I wanted you to know what happened."

I struck out once more for an even more important position. The position of chancellor of the California State Community Colleges was open, and a nationally known talent search firm asked me to apply. The firm thought I was tailor-made for the job. Once again I went through the complicated interview process. I really knew more about community college education in the state than the people interviewing me. They were mostly politicians, and so I had to hold back in order not to embarrass them. Everything went very well, I thought, as I flew home.

I learned a few days later that a black educator from back east had gotten the post. The recruiter from the search team called in great embarrassment. "I was present in all the interviews," he said, "and you were by far the strongest candidate. I don't know what happened." The new chancellor lasted only a couple of years before he resigned rather than be fired.

In these matters, I was swimming upstream at the wrong time, I guess. Maybe I was a threat to some groups who were in a position to stop someone like me. I was an example of many successful Mexican Americans who had not been boosted by affirmative action or special assistance. At Pomona College, Harvard, or anywhere else, I had never received special help for being Mexican. By now I had come to resent affirmative action that served to hurt Mexican Americans rather than help them.

All of these setbacks still hurt, not only for personal reasons but for what they meant for younger Mexican Americans. Had I gained any of these three positions, I would have worked hard to make a national impact for not just Mexican Americans but other students as well. These losses still hurt, especially for the reasons that I lost out.

Looking back, it is hard to believe that I suffered still another frustration in my efforts to gain a university presidency. I applied for the opening at my own campus (Northridge) several years after returning from the embassy in Mexico City. Claudia Hampton was still a member of the statewide board of trustees. I spoke to her frankly about the possibility of applying because her support would be crucial. I figured that out of guilt, as well as from twelve years of collaboration on minority affairs in the school district, she might be willing to help. She blurted out, "Wonderful. You would be just right. Let's strategize." I was delighted because she was chair of the selection committee and could be very influential.

A month passed without my receiving the usual courtesy letter that my application and papers had been received by the committee. Instead of getting an invitation to appear before the search committee, I read an article in the *Los Angeles Times* that Dr. Blenda Wilson, a black educator from out of state had been appointed president. I later learned that Claudia had actually put me down in remarks to Chancellor Barry Munitz by referring to "the age factor." I was 65 years old then. My supporters observed that, whereas most university presidents are appointed younger and age discrimination was illegal, President Ronald Reagan was much older at his first election. State University Chancellor Munitz, for his part, had made very encouraging remarks about me to State Senator Gary Hart, who had supported me warmly. Gary Hart told me that Munitz said, "You will be happy with the results." Hart was chairman of the legislature's State Education Committee, and so the chancellor was compelled to talk frankly with him. I was deceived by the chancellor and betrayed by Claudia once again. A few years later, I heard that Dr. Hampton had died.

All during public life I had turned down offers to make money by doing favors. Some Mexican-American-elected officials have been embarrassed on occasion by selling favors. In this regard, they are no different than others involved in graft. However, such conduct hurts the entire Hispanic community and not simply the family involved. Such conduct also places additional handicaps in the way of progress for our group. Declining offers for graft, the Navas have gotten along on my own earnings only. I earned what we needed, even if not all we wanted. Any one of these lost positions would have made for a very comfortable retirement and a head start for the Nava children.

Chapter 23

Our Ambassadorial Experience in Mexico

One hot valley Saturday, I was mowing the lawn and was flushed with sweat as Pat called out that I was wanted on the telephone. Annoyed at the interruption, I stormed into the kitchen. A stranger asked if I was Dr. Nava, to which I replied, "No, it's Christopher Columbus." The man persisted like a salesman. I was about to hang up, when he asked if my driver's license was Z0303064. Although this caught my attention, and I said yes, I knew that getting such a number is not very hard to do. By now he was slightly annoyed. He said, "Your Social Security number is so and so and your naval air corps service number is 566-97-45, is that not so?" Well, this stumped me because you have to be well connected to government to get that number. My tone changed and so did his.

He told me that my name had come to the attention of the White House as a possible American ambassador to Mexico. If I was interested, the State Department would fly me back to Washington for interviews. However, I could not tell anyone about this conversation in order to avoid embarrassment for the government and myself. Not even my wife could know about this.

Within a week I was flying to Washington, D.C. for a round of interviews with selected members of the Senate, the State Department, President Jimmy Carter's personal staff, and his national security advisor. Everyone was satisfied that I knew Mexico well and spoke Spanish, which the president had insisted upon. My elected public service satisfied everyone that I could function in public life.

On my return to Los Angeles, the Mexican consul invited me to lunch. After much polite conversation about relations between the two governments, we parted. A few days later the Mexican government confidentially gave notice of its acceptance of my designation. If for any reason Mexico voiced reservations, then the American president would have considered carefully whether to proceed with the appointment.

My conversation with California Senator S.I. Hyakawa was one of the more interesting interviews before consideration by the U.S. Senate. His seat was up for election in a year. He asked me very pointedly whether I had intentions to run for the U.S. Senate. When I assured him I had no such intention, he said with relief that Senate approval of my nomination would pose no problem, and it didn't. I gained unanimous consent in the Senate to become the U.S. ambassador to Mexico.

I could now tell Pat what all this activity was about. Her first reaction was "I am not going." But obviously she gave way as she had done when I became a school board candidate. Before long, she was trying to sell three horses, but not her own. We kept Prince and boarded him during our absence. Packing and many such things kept her very busy while I went back to Washington for briefings. The children were both excited and confused. How can you know what lies in store?

My briefings were an eye-opener because most of the information was not publicly known. Every now and then I would ask myself, "What am I doing here? There must be some mistake. This is a dream."

The CIA briefings were especially interesting. After signing papers that I would never reveal the information I was going to receive, we went below ground several floors. Enough time has now gone by that I can reveal how good our satellites' cameras and listening devices were. You could tell whether a Russian on the ground needed a shave and listen in to telephone calls in Moscow or anywhere else, for that matter. I joked about whether we could spot illegal immigrants crossing the Rio Grande at night. "Mr. Ambassador, we can spot a coyote," the agent said. I wondered why we didn't do just that if we were truly serious about stopping illegal immigration. The fact is we were not that serious. On a confidential basis, most Washington officials realized that our economy depended on undocumented labor from Mexico.

By now, everybody was very respectful. Well, almost everyone. A member of the State Department asked me to dinner at his charming home in Washington, D.C. He had been a professor of English history and a specialist on Shakespeare, which made for interesting conversation with good food and wine. However, Robert Kreuger did not tell me that he had been a candidate for the position of ambassador and had been granted a post in the State Department as a consolation prize. We had a pleasant dinner without my knowing what he had done a couple of weeks earlier. It turned out that Kreuger had been the source of a leak to the newspapers of my designation as ambassador, before Senate approval. Kreuger had broken the rules of silence to complicate my Senate confirmation, but the effort had failed. Kreuger suffered handicaps in the State Department after that. The rugs in his office needed replacement, the walls needed painting, and his office space was insufficient.

Something sad happened during the exciting period of confirmation hearings. Two Chicano community leaders with good connections in Washington asked me out for lunch. After much conversation and congratulations, they voiced hope that no skeletons in the closet would derail my nomination. They asked whether I had anything in my past that might cause problems, so that countermeasures might be taken beforehand. I was stunned by the implication of such a question. I kept a poker face as I replied that I could not recall anything embarrassing except some traffic tickets. Anyway, I said with a laugh, after the FBI check of my background, the agency knew more about me than I could remember. I wondered why they would want to know something even the FBI did not know, and the implication saddened me.

Back at the CSUN campus, my good friend Reba Soffer called to tell me she had just vented her wrath to a mutual friend over my appointment. It turned out that during the FBI security check, Reba was asked whether it was true that I made regular trips to Cuba. Another colleague had said, "I don't know why Julian keeps visiting Cuba." The FBI agent was seeking clarification of this statement. Reba said that, yes, I had visited Cuba in 1960, just after the revolution had chased away the dictator Fulgencio Batista, but not again. The agent agreed that the FBI knew I had made only one visit. The FBI also knew that upon my return from Cuba in 1960, I gave numerous talks that were critical of the Cuban Revolution. Reba is so intelligent and has such a sharp tongue that I can only imagine what she said in anger to our mutual friend in the department who had tried to sabotage my appointment.

All the family went to Washington for the ceremony in which I was to take the oath of office, called "swearing in." Several political friends, including the actor Eddie Albert and CEO of Arco Petroleum, Lod Cook, accepted my invitation as well. I liked Eddie's movie and television work. The large number of family and friends from East Los Angeles took the State Department by surprise. We visited with President Carter, whom I now met for the first time. I could tell that, being a Southerner, he just loved the invasion of the White House by the Navas. We took in all the major sights and enjoyed the Smithsonian Institution most of all.

By now, all the major newspapers carried articles on my appointment. Our embassy in Mexico City is larger than those in London, Paris, or Moscow, and the appointment to Mexico is very newsworthy. The volume and importance of the work there explains the size of the embassy, and therefore, our ambassador there commands attention. Who he is and what he does affects American interests.

While Pat and the children returned home to pack, I stayed on for briefings. My sister Rosemarie, whom we all called "Honey" since childhood, solved one big problem. She and her husband Chuck simply locked up their house nearby and moved into ours. In this way, we had to pack only personal belongings and the dogs.

I went to Mexico ahead of the family. A huge mariachi band and a dozen reporters and TV cameras were waiting for me at the Mexico City airport. The U.S. embassy staff was there to greet their new boss, and they were thrown off balance by the crowd. The happy Mexican music blasted at full throttle as I walked out of the loading tunnel, and I was thrown off balance myself. John Ferch, my future deputy chief of mission, walked up with his wife and yelled, "Welcome to Mexico, Mr. Ambassador."

I just stood there accepting greetings from embassy staff, and then the music stopped. Suddenly, we could speak in a normal tone. On the sidelines of the crowd, I could see our cousin Miguel Flores smiling from ear to ear, and then I guessed what had happened. While the embassy had not announced my arrival, Miguel had tipped off the press. John agreed we might as well talk to the media, whom the airport police was holding back.

The press asked many questions, some that I could not answer at the time. My reply to one question was reported widely on TV and in print. Quite often, U.S. ambassadors leave their family home and visit them from abroad. More often than not, their children stay at school and visit with their fathers abroad. Some countries take this practice as a sign of lack of confidence for security in the country where the ambassador is working. There was the hint of this when one fellow asked why my family did not accompany me. I explained that they were hard at work packing, but that Pat, our three children, and the three dogs would soon be in Mexico. The Mexican news media loved it that even the dogs were coming.

Before the family arrived, I spent the time getting acquainted with the thousand or so staff at the embassy on the beautiful Paseo de la Reforma. Due to a death in the family of the Mexican president, the formal visits to each foreign embassy were held off until the mourning period was over. There is a very strict sequence for these visits, according to tradition. Such visits must start with the president, then members of his cabinet, and only then the other ambassadors, according to the length of their residence in the capital. The most senior ambassador was a charming woman from Panama.

In order to meet personally all the embassy staff, I started from the basement floors of the building (don't ask how many) to the rooftop, where the CIA had its radio transmission tower and telephone interception equipment. It turned out that no U.S. ambassador in memory had ever gone to this trouble, and the gesture was greatly appreciated by embassy staff. There was no hope that I could remember all those names, but each employee sure remembered mine.

Several said they had worked at the embassy during several ambassadors, but I was the first they had ever met in person. Except for key U.S. staff, the employees were Mexican citizens. All could speak perfect English. When I spoke in Spanish to the Mexicans, you could see pride sparkle in their eyes. I really think this move raised performance in the staff. For my part, it was just good politics.

While these ordinary Mexican folks were proud to meet the first U.S. ambassador of Mexican descent, not all upper-class people in Mexican society shared this feeling. They seemed to wonder how a Mexican American from a poor family could gain this position. They were used to dealing with millionaire ex-presidents of huge corporations with high social standing. I could sense these feelings as I met these upper-class Mexicans at social affairs. I could sense that they were polite because they had to be.

Gradually, this snobbish reception gave way as I appeared on television, and it became common knowledge that I had attended such insider colleges as Pomona and Harvard University and spoke Spanish fluently. Now and then I got the chance to explain that other "méxico-americanos" were commonly enrolled at such campuses on the basis of merit and not just money or family connections. I wanted people to know that there were many Mexican Americans like me. I had private scorn for snobbish Mexicans because I knew that some of them had inherited wealth or social standing from graft in government. Their children could study in Europe or the finest schools in the United States, if they chose. However, in the event a Mexican youth aspired to a political career, a degree from a Mexican public university was essential. Notwithstanding my early biases, some of the best friends we made in Mexico happened to be wealthy.

My ambassadorial speechwriter was a Jewish American

named Stan. Stan knew all about me by means of the American Jewish grapevine, which is very efficient. He knew I was raised among Jews in East L.A. and worked in politics closely with the Jewish community. Stan was not surprised that our family was happy to join the Jewish country club. The beautiful grounds, golf course, swimming pools, and other facilities made a great weekend retreat for the family. Actually, we went only a few times because of our busy schedule. When the aristocratic Mexicans of the Chapultepec Country Club learned what I had done, I gained a unique distinction among American ambassadors. All American ambassadors before us had been given membership in this club, except me. Anti-Semitism is still strong among many upper-class Mexicans. For them, I had committed a social sin by accepting an invitation to join the Jewish country club.

I got along fine with President José López Portillo, in part because he was a university professor and very intelligent, though not wealthy. This shortcoming was overcome overwhelmingly while he was president. His sister became notorious for graft, as did most of his administration. Compared to previous governments, his gained the reputation of being the most corrupt. As a taxi driver said to me after I left the post, "We know they all steal, but why so much?"

The president made a very nice gesture at the ceremonies in which I presented my credentials from President Jimmy Carter. Pat, Henry, and I went past an honor guard at the presidential palace in the giant plaza called El Zócalo. The huge government buildings and the beautiful cathedral built during colonial times sit right over the center of the Aztec capital, as if to show that Spaniards had conquered the Mexicans. When we strolled down the long halls to the president's office, hundreds of school children lined the walls, waving hello to a teacher. When I stopped to say hello to some, their big black eyes just beamed up at me.

The president and his foreign minister, Jorge Castañeda, and I chatted nonsense while the photographers did their thing. The president then asked me what plans I had now that I was in Mexico. He burst out laughing when I whispered, "Well, Mr. President, I don't really know, since I am new at this job." The foreign minister could not hear my reply, but he laughed because the president laughed. The photographers did their thing all over again, since these ceremonies are always serious affairs. The three of us chatted and got to know each other. Pat and Henry were just out of earshot, standing on one foot and then another. Other ambassadors waited outside, wondering about the delay before presenting their credentials.

Immediately after leaving President López Portillo, I was surrounded by newspaper reporters, and I demonstrated that I really did know what I was going to do as ambassador. Although given wide latitude by President Carter and the U.S. Secretary of State, I was given some specific instructions. One of the things I was supposed to do was to make public American disappointment that President López Portillo had at the last minute changed his mind and decided that Mexico would not join the General Agreement on Trade and Tariffs, or GATT. This international understanding would take bold steps to regulate international trade, limiting the freedom of individual countries in trade matters for the benefit of all the members. When questioned by a crowd of reporters in the Presidential Palace, I said that the United States was saddened by Mexico's unexpected change in policy. The United States would respect the decision, of course, I said, but certain trade consequences would arise as Mexico stayed out of the new international trading family. The Mexican press seized on the word "consequences" and made it appear that I was threatening Mexico on behalf of

President Carter.

The Mexican president was disturbed by my remarks, just as we were disturbed by Mexico's isolationist position. In diplomacy, it is often tit for tat. I got no reprimand from Washington for my remarks, and within Mexico there emerged the clear impression that the Chicano ambassador would speak out plainly on bilateral relations. Even if his family was from Zacatecas, Ambassador Nava was American.

When I visited Secretary of Foreign Relations Jorge Castañeda at his offices high in a skyscraper, he kept talking to me in English even though I spoke to him in Spanish. I figured I should use Spanish since I was in Mexico, but he maintained the conversation in English. I was annoyed. I figured it would stay this way until the end of the protocol visit, his talking in English and my replying in Spanish. Then a jolly Mexican lady came in with coffee and Mexican bread, which I never got enough of as a boy. She heard me talking in Spanish and replied to my warm thanks. Normally, it was not my place to engage a servant in conversation nor for her to reply, but we exchanged a few remarks. She said it was a pleasure to converse at last with an American ambassador in Spanish. When she left, Castañeda switched to Spanish for the rest of my visit. A few weeks later, he invited me to have lunch at his home, where I met his wife, who our files described as Russian-born and a Marxist. The three of us had a delightful time, which my staff said was out of the ordinary because Castañeda was proud, aloof, and rarely had visits from ambassadors at home.

Mexico's new confidence, stemming from huge petroleum discoveries, complicated bilateral relations and made all discussions more difficult. Jorge Díaz Serrano, head of the government petroleum monopoly PEMEX, kept announcing new discoveries of oil on land and in the Gulf of Mexico. Our spy network confirmed these announcements and tried to reconcile them with the limits on oil sales to the United States that Mexico was establishing. President López Portillo summed up the government's attitude by proudly stating in public that Mexico's only problems now were dealing with abundance. For the first time in its history, Mexico seemed to have the advantage over the colossus to the north. We learned that Díaz Serrano had such voluminous offers to buy Mexican oil that they were stacked on the floor. Offers of American oil companies to buy at almost any price were piled with the others and got no special treatment.

Lod Cook, CEO of Arco Petroleum, came to Mexico to deal firsthand with the Mexicans in PEMEX (Petróleos Mexicanos). We hosted him in the ambassadorial residence and started a long-lasting friendship. Like others, he went home with empty hands in view of a Mexican practice to always say yes, but never when.

Mexico enjoyed having the advantage over the United States on energy issues. How did this come about? The Arab oil producers were united in a group called OPEC, Organization of Petroleum Exporting Countries. This international cartel—the brainchild of a Venezuelan, by the way—fixed production quotas, sales volume, and prices. Due to OPEC, the Western nations, such as France, England, Holland, and the United States, lost control over oil in the producing countries, despite their having cooperated with Middle Eastern countries in exploration and refining.

Angry with what Arabs considered unfair Western support for Israel, OPEC stopped selling oil selectively to some Western countries and compensated for the loss of volume by raising the prices for the rest of the world. Although the "Arab oil boycott," as it was called, started in the latter part of the Richard Nixon and Gerald Ford administrations, the impact finally hit hard during the Jimmy Carter administration (1976–1980). Many American factories were forced to close down, producing massive unemployment and a drastic reduction of federal revenues.

I had the job of persuading Mexico to increase its oil sales to our country. I had plenty of help from Washington, but I was onpoint, as they say in the military. Nothing would change Mexico's mind, and in fact, its position hardened. President Carter was very worried about the stagnation in the economy as the price of oil rose about fourfold. This increase made everything produced or transported with energy increase in price. Gasoline rose from about 25 cents a gallon to well over a dollar, a level it has not dropped from even after supplies were restored.

President Carter started worrying about reelection, as well as the economy. Mexico just smiled at our problems. Soon after these economic problems worsened, Carter allowed the industrial use of our military oil reserves stored in deep caves underground. Mexico found out about this and stated strongly that if any U.S. oil company bought Mexican oil with the secret intentions of transferring it to the strategic reserves, that company would never again obtain Mexican oil.

I explained to the Mexican government that in view of the Cold War, our strategic reserves could not be reduced to the point that national security was endangered. Why was President Carter using these reserves for domestic purposes? Our economy was slowing down so dangerously that we could not cope with the new conditions. We had always enjoyed an ample supply of oil at low prices, but now prices for everything were rising, even as employment was rising with less production. Just about everyone was suffering from the consequences of the Arab oil boycott, including poor countries everywhere. Third World countries suffered more than we did. Their economies were less able to withstand the shock of the higher oil prices.

In the past, consumer prices had gone down during a recession, but this time they were going up, due to the cost of energy. This new situation was called "stagflation," because there was inflation in prices during a stagnation of the economy. American oil companies were making so much money from the oil price increases that they didn't know what to do with it. Arab government bank deposits all over the world were upsetting the economy. Banks could not find enough borrowers of their huge new holdings. Banks everywhere made many bad loans as a result. Swiss banks, as usual, knew what to do. They accepted Arab money for safekeeping, but paid no interest on the deposits, and, in fact, they charged fees for safekeeping.

Mexicans said they were not concerned about President Carter's reelection, and that, in any case, Mexico was not involved in the Cold War. In fact, López Portillo was spending millions in public relations abroad to become a leader in the so-called Third World. These nations that foolishly claimed they were not involved in the struggle between the Western democracies and the communists were looking for leadership—as well as oil supplies. Mexico seemed like their answer. In view of all this, Mexico made only very modest increases in oil sales to us, setting its prices only slightly below OPEC. This did not help our economy much. PEMEX officials at all levels became extremely wealthy as potential buyers paid bribes merely to gain consideration of their purchase offers.

Without presidential authority, a group of high U.S. military officers came to visit me with an astounding request. They wanted me to approve U.S. naval exercises in international waters off the coast of Veracruz. For a former lowly naval petty officer third class like me to be in the company of several admirals was impressive. For the first time, it struck me as never before that in Mexico I had the authority of the American president. I knew it in my mind beforehand, but now I was living it. These folks were going to use live ammunition exercises within earshot of the port. Sixteen-inch naval guns can be heard for many miles.

Our discussions took place at the residence. At the end of their first presentation, I suggested we meet again the next day, after I met with my cabinet. All the cabinet members were opposed to the project and left it to me to say no. At the residence over cocktails, the admirals and I repeated our opposing positions several times. They had brought along a Mexican-American rear admiral who tried to use our relationship as a lever, but it was to no avail. Finally I said that my opposition would not change, but that should they want to go above me, they could of course ask the president to give me instructions. I had never seen such hard stares focused on me as they took their leave. I never heard of their project again, which convinced me that they were acting on their own and without presidential backing. They clearly were trying to scare Mexico into selling more oil to us, and the proximity of Veracruz drove the threat home. The United States had used Veracruz as a route to invade Mexico in the last century. The rear admiral later got the award of the Aztec Eagle, Mexico's highest civilian award for civic virtues, because the fellow acted publicly like a great friend of Mexico. I just shook my head at hearing this news and remembered how strange politics can be sometimes.

I sensed some initial reservations about me among my cabinet at the embassy because I was a political appointee. This group of about twenty represented all the departments in the presidential cabinet. Each of these had regular contact with his corresponding cabinet members. Some cabinet members, however, carried out their own policies in Mexico, regardless of State Department policy because there had been a lapse of time between the departure of my predecessor and my appointment. Sometimes these folks worked against each other, reflecting rivalry among cabinet members.

John Ferch, my assistant and a State Department professional, advised me to get complete control early in the game or lose it thereafter, like other ambassadors had. At a weekly cabinet meeting, I seized control of my team by offering rewards or punishment for loyalty. I rendered a highly political talk, admitting that as a political appointee, I would come and go while they would stay on. My success depended upon their loyal support, I stated. However, I pointed out clearly that their career advancement depended on my confidential evaluation of their performance. They knew that I had already given an example of what I could do. I had ordered the transfer of my State Department personal secretary to some other embassy of her choice because the chemistry between us was not right. This was a setback to her career plans, and they knew it. Actually, they were glad she was gone. I concluded by saying, "You can help me best by telling me just what you believe, rather than what you think will please me. You help me do well, and I will help you move ahead in the foreign service." That took care of the problem of staff loyalty and my leadership.

Some of our meetings were very confidential. In the regular meeting room, we feared that Russian listening posts could overhear us, and so we spoke in general and guarded language. For certain discussions we met in the bubble room. That was a room within a room within a room. This location was completely secure from outside listeners. No listening device could break in. I always had claustrophobia in this small room and tried to get to the point right away. Of course, we ourselves listened in on the Russians, the Mexicans, and other major foreign embassies. We assumed that other embassies tried to listen in on our embassy to the best of their ability.

Our embassy was completely self-sufficient, with water, food, and other supplies in case of a siege. In Iran, the U.S. embassy had been seized and all the staff made prisoners, to the great embarrassment of the U.S. government. Nothing President Carter tried would gain their release. Iranians had good reasons to be unhappy with the United States historically, and President Carter had only made matters worse by giving assistance to the ruler of Iran when a popular revolution overthrew him. President Carter's Christian humanity led him to obtain medical treatment for the dying Shah of Iran, instead of turning him over for trial and certain death at the hands of the Muslims who now ran the Iranian government. We took new precautions to avoid the possibility of an attack on the embassy, even though we were in a friendly country. The embassy was occasionally surrounded by demonstrations of Mexicans. I don't recall another embassy in Mexico being subjected to as many loud protests as ours. We never forgot that the seizure of the American embassy in Tehran was the product of a university student demonstration that got out of hand, and that the Iranian government had supported it to save face among the masses. Our small contingent of marines at the embassy in Mexico was always on guard, and I never went anywhere at the same time or by the same route two times in a row. My armored Chrysler sedan was so heavy it required a brake job every three weeks.

Since the young marines were sworn to protect me and my family at all cost, I concluded they deserved special attention. Much to their surprise, I spent an afternoon in their barracks-like home, drinking beer and comparing stories about military service. I must have drunk about ten beers to maintain naval honor in the face of this marine detachment. In the navy, there is a traditional rivalry and a polite mutual disdain between sailors and marines. After this display of deference on my part, the gallant young marines seemed to stand up even taller when they saluted me at the embassy.

On the roof of the embassy building, the CIA ran its listening post that could cut into just about any telephone conversation in Mexico City. Only they and I could go into that post. I believe that our abilities in this area were better than those of the Russians, but how could we be sure? Every country spied on every other one and did not reveal its findings.

I recall the briefing on our listening capabilities, which I had received at CIA headquarters in Virginia. It was not obvious, but Mexico City was at the heart of the Cold War because it was Russia's main access to the United States for espionage. The Soviet bloc ran its spies, exchanges of information, and money through Mexico because our border is so porous. They knew we knew all this, and the CIA was in the middle of the tug-of-war. I recall seeing photos of Russian cities and some close-ups of cars and people. License plates and personal identification were no problem, unless it was cloudy as our satellites passed over on their regular orbits. Fifteen years later when I visited some of these cities in Siberia, I looked up and wondered if our satellites were still looking down. I think so, because communists are still entrenched in government everywhere in post-communist Russia.

Our ordinary telephones could probably be overheard by the Russians, so we made important calls to Washington in a special soundproof room using a safe phone. When you spoke slowly and clearly, the sender phone distorted the sound transmission into a meaningless noise that kept changing at random as you spoke. The receiver phone unscrambled the sounds, and your phone did the same when listening to the reply. Cables (like telegrams) went by air from the rooftop in scrambled form that was printed out at the receiving end. Original letters went by special mail carriers, but these took a couple of days in each direction.

The station chief of the CIA invited me to use its own form of communication back and forth to Washington, but I declined politely, although it was better than the system I described above. There was a constant rivalry between the State Department and the CIA. Each did not want the other to know what they were doing, except when necessary. Each decided when it was necessary. I could not let the CIA have full knowledge of sensitive communications between the embassy and the State Department.

The nice man in charge of the CIA and I met weekly, so he could brief me on whatever he learned through their various sources of information. These sources included Mexicans from all walks of life, including some in very high government positions that were on the payroll of the CIA. The station chief was known only to me and John Ferch. Everyone else in the embassy thought he was just another staff member. Even today I cannot reveal his name. We got along fine and occasionally went to the same Protestant church, where he arranged for me to give a sort of a sermon one Sunday evening.

What strange rules of the game we played by. The station chief hinted that he would feel more comfortable if Ferch was not in the weekly briefings because he was a State Department foreign service officer. John was annoyed, but accepted my suggestion that we please the chief so that I would get the fullest amount of information. John and I could later have a cup of coffee, and I could brief him. You see, John was in a position to evaluate some things better than I, and besides, this technique assured the State Department that I was a loyal member of its team. If my station chief friend ever guessed what I was doing, he never let on. It was part of the game.

What a strange coincidence that John Ferch had a job like the one I dreamed about while attending East Los Angeles Community College (1947–1949). When I mentioned the hope of becoming a foreign service officer to my career advisor, both he and the college librarian advised me to set aside that lofty goal. The foreign service was traditionally very aristocratic, they said, and did not have minorities in it. It was made up of white, Anglo-Saxon males from "good families" who attended private colleges in the East. As I looked around at my embassy staff, this pattern still held true in 1980. In spite of all this, here I was as an ambassador rather than simply a foreign service officer, as I had dreamed about thirty years earlier.

John Ferch was first rate in every respect. Upon leaving the post, I sent in the strongest recommendation that he was ready to be a full ambassador. And sure enough, I learned later that he was assigned to a Central American republic, but that his service there did not last long. As the administration of President Ronald Reagan began its illegal efforts to overthrow the communist government in Nicaragua, people around Reagan began to subvert John's country, so to speak. Huge amounts of money for bribery and for military equipment were moved into that country to make it a base of operations against Nicaragua. John's reports back to the State Department displeased the Reagan administration, and John was demoted to a desk job in the State Department. I lost track of John, but hoped his career would recover under another administration. This was doubtful because President George Bush, who followed Reagan into the White House, was formerly head of the CIA and as vice president under Reagan was a key person in the illegal war against Nicaragua, even if he denied it publicly.

Some of that make-believe experience affected family life. Poor Pat, she did a good job at something she did not really like. All the ceremonies and receptions were boring to her as she made polite conversation with complete strangers. One of these occasions made me especially proud. When I introduced Pat to the Mexican president, he spoke in Spanish, of course. He expected me to translate for her, but Pat replied in the crisp, correct Spanish she had acquired living in Valladolid. It surprised the president and the foreign secretary that this blonde *gringa* was speaking as well as they.

The news media in Mexico was dominated by the government. Our family was warmly treated, but I was in hot water regularly. The government set out a policy line on certain issues, and reporters wrote stories that reinforced the government position. Sometimes the stories were clearly incorrect. Important reporters regularly got envelopes stuffed with cash from someone in the government and they relied on this subsidy. A reporter did not have to accept these tips, but if he didn't play by the rules, he would soon be out of a job. This was one way the Mexican government controlled the news and, therefore, public opinion in Mexico. The supply of newspapers was another form of control. The government owned most suppliers of newsprint paper and denied paper to newspapers and magazines that were too independent of the government political line. Artificial delays in deliveries were enough to punish print media to be more cooperative in reporting on government policy.

I was in Monterey delivering a speech to businessmen when an assistant came up and whispered that so and so had just died. I said, "Good, now he will be off our backs." This guy was a communist labor leader and was always giving the United States a bad time in the press. The problem with him was that he was often right in what he said, although he exaggerated greatly.

Stan had a bright idea to blunt some of the violent press attacks on the United States. Why didn't I go to his wake? These *velorios*, as the wakes are called, go on all night before the burial, as family and friends stop by to pay their last respects. Having telephoned for an order of a huge wreath of flowers with a large banner reading "From the American Ambassador," we took a midnight flight. A huge crowd waited in the street to enter his humble home. The large crowd parted like the Red Sea, and we went right in. I made a ceremonial visit to the open casket. I whispered, "Well, here you are, you son of a bitch." I then went over to the widow sitting among her children. She was amazed to see me. She was so tired, and her eyes were red and dry. I bent over and whispered to her sincerely that while I had rarely agreed with her husband in political matters, I always respected him as a great Mexican patriot. She burst out crying again as I walked out through the crowd into the morning light. After that event, the leftist press in Mexico softened its attacks on me, although not on the United States.

I was the object of many cartoons, some of them comical and others rather offensive. I saw these in the daily staff clippings of every article that dealt with the United States in the twelve capital newspapers. One day my secretary Carmen Orozco and I were laughing at one cartoon at my expense. The two of us had worked together for the many years I was on the school board. Carmen thought of inviting the artist to visit for a cup of coffee and requested that he bring the original cartoon drawing, if he would be so kind. Much to my surprise, one after another cartoonists accepted the odd invitation. I have a collection of these cartoons in the hallway. Each has to do with a hot political issue of the time. I must say, the artists were surprised that the target of their satire asked them over for coffee and laughed with them at the ironies of public life.

The protocol visits to all the ambassadors were sometimes interesting, but they were usually dull. Before each visit, I would get a briefing on that country and the ambassador so that we would have something to talk about. I ran into a bit of a buzz saw with the French ambassador. He was well educated, aristocratic, and subtly arrogant and ethnocentric. Actually, the French have so much to be proud of. Their food, style in dress, music, literature, and all the rest are first class. I made the mistake of speaking to him in French. After a short pause, he politely suggested we speak in English. His English with a slight British accent was perfect, while my French was only basic. I could tell he at least appreciated that I was educated and not simply a wealthy American businessman or politician paid off with an ambassadorial appointment. My predecessor could not speak Spanish, and so this slowed down everything in U.S.-Mexican relations.

The visit to the Panamanian ambassador was delightful in contrast to the French. This beautiful lady was charming and very intelligent. As dean of the diplomatic corps—the longest serving in Mexico—she knew that I had instructions not to visit the Cuban embassy. This led to a long conversation about my experience in Cuba when the revolution had put an end to the regime of Fulgencio Batista. She told me delightful stories about her very dear friend Fidel Castro and how things were in Cuba, where she visited from time to time.

The Soviet bloc countries were giving a lot of money to Cuba during this time and trading with it on terms that were, in effect, a subsidy. Soviet bloc arms and advisors were everywhere in Cuba, although Cubans generally did not like them. The United States was opposed to the Cuban regime and could not forget that Castro had intended to install Russian missiles on the island in 1962. I expressed the view that the installation of missiles was understandable after our effort to invade Cuba and overthrow Castro a year earlier. I went on that Cubans were a remarkable people and that I hoped our relations could become more normal for mutual benefit. Her big black eyes opened wider, and she said, "You are not an ordinary American ambassador."

I guessed that she reported my remarks to Havana.

Upon my return to the embassy, I wrote up notes on the visit, as usual. I urged the White House to soften its embargo on trade with Cuba as a more effective way to undermine the communist influence. It's possible that the conversation with the Panamanian ambassador helped me in 1996 to gain Cuban permission to film a documentary in Cuba. Governments take note of all such conversations and look them up later when the need arises.

I once stated to the press that Americans were confused that a democratic nation like Mexico was so friendly with a communist nation like Cuba. I caught hell in the Mexican press for interfering in the internal affairs of Mexico. This prompted mean cartoons at my expense. I just laughed off the reporters' questions by saying that my frankness was simply proof of the friendly relations between our two countries. I observed we could speak frankly about matters of mutual concern, like a husband and wife. That prompted a cartoon the next day showing a tall Uncle Sam hugging a short señorita with lust in his eyes. The caption read, "Please Mr. Ambassador, don't be so graphic!" Mexicans generally love humor, especially political satire. I figure that Mexicans love political satire because it helps them cope with conditions that would be unbearable otherwise.

I found many occasions to use humor with the Mexican press because humor would let me say something I should not say seriously. There was the case of the terrible drought that was hurting Mexican agriculture while I was there. Some Mexican newspapers carried stories that U.S. scientists were seeding the clouds to prevent rain in Mexico out of revenge for Mexico's refusal to sell more oil to the United States. I stated to the news media very solemnly that the United States was afflicted by incompetence, graft, and deceit like other countries I knew. Any criminals seeding clouds to divert rainfall should be sent to prison, since they were responsible for causing the same drought that afflicted our entire Midwest, as well as Mexico. Reporters started to smile and then laugh out loud when they caught on to my implications. The cloud-seeding story died.

One of my principal tasks was to help American businessmen in Mexico because their success helped create jobs in the United States. All U.S. ambassadors have this assignment. What this amounted to for me was to join the American Chamber of Commerce, whose membership included all the important U.S. businesspeople. I gave speeches to the Chamber and its chapters in several Mexican cities. My speechwriter would work up a draft of my remarks, which I would revise. He would then polish the speech and enrich it with the latest information.

One of the more interesting chores was to intercede on behalf of American companies when some Mexican agency or government official was not treating the American company fairly. I remember the case of a large American maker of electrical equipment who wanted to make a huge sale to Mexico. It turns out that the Mexican government was going to buy the equipment from a French firm, partly owned by the French government. The French price for comparable equipment was lower than the American's because the French government was giving a subsidy to the French firm to undersell the Americans. There was also a payoff to high-up Mexican officials, which was illegal for the American firm to make under our laws. When the company representative and I met with the Mexican president, I told him about the French government subsidy. The president was surprised I knew about the secret subsidy, but he did not ask how I knew about it. I casually pointed out that if all governments played this way, international trade would be harmed. More important, Mexico and the United States were major trading partners and would want to avoid becoming involved in a game that both countries could play. Besides, as neighbors we could offer better and quicker servicing of the railroad equipment in question. This better service would offset the lower French costs. He just smiled and said he would do what he could.

Some time later, the U.S. company representative called and simply said over the phone, "Mr. Ambassador, I am authorized to tell you that should you need anything at all that we can provide in the future, you can just call us." I never did. This offer faded away like others that could have made the Navas wealthy. However, I can sleep well with no fear about embarrassing disclosures about my service as ambassador.

Another example of helping American business was the series of weekly meetings with about twenty of the top CEOs of American businesses. This was a novel idea of the embassy commercial officer, which I quickly accepted. The rules for the meetings in the ambassador's residence were that no written notes or recordings were to be made and the list of those attending was confidential. Over fine scotch and Cuban cigars (easy to get in Mexico), we talked about conditions in commerce. Each gave the others the latest news. This proved to be very helpful to each of the companies. The commercial officer and I just remembered it all, wrote it up, and cabled the information to Washington. Nothing like that had been done before, and the businesspeople, as well as the State Department, were happy about it.

Now and then matters came up that were very enjoyable, like the decision of the Association of Mexican-American Educators to hold its annual convention in Mexico City for the first time. My presence in Mexico served as an excuse to bring together about eight hundred members from all over the Southwest. We had a gala reception at the ambassador's residence and got a lot of news coverage. All this helped inform well-placed Mexicans that not all Mexican Americans were farmworkers. The *charreada* the group planned was rained out, so we met in a nearby barn and danced the night away to authentic Mexican food, margaritas, and mariachis.

Toward the end of our stay, the Navas had a pleasant encounter with the Russian ambassador. At one of those countless receptions at the residence, the diplomatic corps showed up for our President's Day reception. No embassy would fail to show up for the American President's Day reception. I recited one of those standard speeches from the lovely spiral staircase. Looking down, I spotted the Russian ambassador, and this reminded me that our holiday was very close to that of a great victory of the Russian armies over the Germans in 1945. The inspiration struck me to say that not only the United States had great leaders, but that we should not forget the terrible sacrifices and bravery of the Russian people, with whom we fought alongside during the struggle against German and Japanese fascism. I went on to say that as high school students, we learned the names of such Russian generals as Zukov and Timoschenko and followed them through movie newsreels reporting on the enormous battles on the Eastern front. Now, in spite of our differences, we were struggling to preserve peace and promote happiness for all. What I said was all true, and so everyone clapped extra loud as I finished and strode down the stairs to receive greetings.

The Russian ambassador pushed through the crowd and took my right hand in both of his. He said that never in his diplomatic career had he heard such generous remarks from an American ambassador. He was obviously moved, I could tell from his voice. He muttered that he was at my service in the Soviet Union. Recovering my own composure, I said that I wondered if he could help me with a dream I had held for many years. I had always wanted to travel on the Transiberian Railroad from Leningrad on the Baltic to Vladivostok on the Pacific. "Done!" he boomed out in a baritone voice. "Just tell me when, and I will see to your accommodations as a state guest." Well, it's sad but true that I could not persuade Pat to accept the offer extended to all of us. I still regret the chance for us to journey these 6,000 miles to exotic lands and peoples as official guests. Fifteen years later, I would fly alone to Siberia, but by then the Soviet Union had broken apart and life there was very unsettled.

The Chinese delegation, as well as the Russian, lived in their own private residential communities. Their staffs rarely went out into Mexico City. President Carter had just reopened an American embassy in Beijing after many years. The very bold idea had been hatched by President Richard Nixon and Secretary of State Henry Kissinger. They figured that contacts were better than isolation. New relations might encourage a Chinese split with the Soviet Union. Our policy makers lost sleep over the possibility that in spite of border controversies, these two communist giants might form a bloc against us.

The Chinese ambassador was probably under instructions to be nice to me in view of President Carter's actions. At a splendid dinner at the Chinese embassy he pulled me aside to a separate room for polite conversation in English. After I praised the wonderful Chinese food, including many dishes I had never tasted in our Los Angeles Chinatown, we got down to politics. We both stated the positions of our governments on certain issues, as if these were a recorded message.

At one point, I said, "Your Excellency, now that we have played our roles, would you like to talk as two ordinary men?" He smiled down at me and agreed. You see, I knew from my briefing on him that he was of the Han people of northern China, and that was why he was so tall and large. Not fat, just very large. I guessed he had a briefing on me, too. We had a delightful discussion, mostly about U.S. politics, since I was very weak on Chinese politics. After this personal acquaintance, we sought each other out during national holiday receptions in one embassy after another. When I sought permission to film a documentary on China about fifteen years later, much to my surprise, I got permission and wide latitude for free movement. I wonder if the Chinese ambassador had sent back nice reports on me.

All the time in Mexico I worried about the safety of my family. All U.S. ambassadors were being alerted to possible terrorist acts against them and their families. The Iranians had seized the U.S. embassy staff in Tehran, and other countries, such as Libya, threatened the United States as well. The newest on the list of terrorists were based in Colombia. While the U.S. ambassador was provided tight security, his family was not, unless they were in his company. I was already in Mexico when I learned how serious the terrorist situation was. I did not inform Pat or the children, other than to tell them to routinely follow all instructions on safety they received from embassy staff. I was very upset that the Department of State did not supply protection for my family, as they did for me. This concern was enough to make me consider resigning, unless protection was provided for Pat and the children. What made me feel better was the remark of President López Portillo: "Enjoy your stay in Mexico, and don't worry; we will take good care of all of you." The host country is responsible for the safety of foreign embassy staff; so my safety was Mexico's responsibility. Very early in our stay, the chief of police for the federal district visited me to assure me that, in keeping with the president's instructions, he would have all the family under constant watch.

All of a sudden it made sense to me that right after the public announcement of my appointment, General Arturo Durazo just happened to be in Los Angeles to receive some honor from the Los Angeles City Council. Through friends, he sought me out, and we established cordial relations. The protective watch over us had started before we arrived in Mexico. I simply knew he was chief of police in Mexico City, but could not imagine how much I would depend on him later.

After a talk with General Durazo in Mexico City, I had staff give me a briefing on the general. It was many pages long. He wasn't really a general, but everyone called him that because he was a lifetime personal friend of the president and could do whatever he wanted. His file was not flattering, but I accepted his protection because it was more than the embassy was equipped to supply for my family. Moreover, in view of his shady past, I figured he would know right away if there was anything to worry about.

General Durazo and his beautiful wife were always overwhelmingly polite and helpful. They lived in a palatial home on a hill overlooking the capital. The indoor basketball court had a floor that could be pulled back to uncover a swimming pool. The very expensive furnishings were not to Pat's taste, but then Pat has very good taste in home furnishings. We did like his horses, however. During a supper at his home, a first-rate mariachi serenaded us with old and classical Mexican music. I had heard a hundred mariachis by this time, but this was probably the best I had ever heard.

Carmen and Katie liked the American school they attended, while Paul found the adjustment to Mexico a little hard to make. The private school our children attended held the children of well-to-do folks who wanted their kids to study in English. The American school devoted much personal attention to the students, and the parents were very involved in school life. Tutoring was available because all students were expected to do very well in their studies.

One of the stories about the children's life there stands out. The girls' volleyball team was in the playoffs for the federal district championship with their traditional rivals across town. It was three games out of five, and the stadium was packed. The teams were evenly matched, so the championship came down to the last game. Just as in a Hollywood movie, the deciding game was down to match point. Purely by chance, Carmen served for the team and Katie was at the net. After numerous vicious exchanges, a player set up Katie, who then spiked the ball for point, game, and match. I am sure they have not forgotten that occasion. Everyone at school liked the twins, and they had fun because they were hard to tell apart until Carmen cut her hair short while Katie kept hers long.

Paul and I took to building remote control model airplanes, which we flew on most Sundays way out in the country with some Mexicans who were not part of the embassy community. We had met a delightful older man at a hobby shop. We were glad that he was not impressed with my position. He taught Paul the basics of flying. I served only as a partner in building the planes because I wanted Paul to learn how to do something better than I. After flying all day Sunday, the dozen pilots and their families had a barbecue out on the field and enjoyed the day until sunset. I rarely let embassy business interfere with this.

Chapter 24

A New Ambassador

President Carter was not reelected in 1980, and so staff at the embassy wondered whether I would be kept on. General Alexander Haig, who was the initial Secretary of State in the new Reagan administration, sent out cables to all the Carter appointees, asking them to leave their posts immediately, as if they were soldiers. Staff said this was brutal treatment and unheard of before. Only two Carter appointees did not get these cables: our ambassador in Tokyo and I. One very prominent American businessman told me that the American Chamber of Commerce wrote to the Secretary of State asking that I be kept on due to my service to the business community.

The fellow who related this to me, Victor, was most interesting. I had been a guest at his house several times at meetings with business folks. On one occasion when we were conversing alone about military service during the Second World War, he went on to tell me that he had been the lead mechanic on the preparation of the Enola Gay. None of his friends in Mexico knew about this. The Enola Gay had dropped the atomic bomb on Hiroshima and then on Nagasaki on a second long flight. Since I had been a naval aviation mechanic myself, Victor went into details about how the Enola Gay was stripped down before the flight. Military planes built on an assembly line often had bugs. His mechanics took the plane apart in a secret location and put it back together again so that nothing would go wrong on that historic flight. He had no misgivings about dropping the bomb, although we both wondered about life in the Atomic Age. I strongly pleaded with him to write his memoirs, but to no avail. Victor died a few years later without writing about the important chapter in history he had experienced.

While my position was up in the air, I met President-elect Ronald Reagan at an El Paso banquet with President López Portillo. I got along fine with Reagan's advance staff, all of whom were Californians. We had some friends in common, chiefly Stu Spencer and Bill Orozco, a personal friend of Reagan's since his governorship of California. Bill's sister, Carmen Orozco Whitehead, was my personal secretary at the embassy. Carmen was like a member of our family and knew what I was going to say before I said it.

Reagan gave President López Portillo a beautiful hunting rifle, which made the president's eyes open wide. Some months later, López Portillo gave Reagan a stallion like few in the world. While visiting the Mexican presidential residence, called Los Pinos, López Portillo had given me a tour of his stables and told me he had turned down an offer of $200,000 for a stallion he had bred. It was the stallion he later gave to Reagan.

I got involved in trying to get the horse into California. The American government agencies would not cooperate to let the horse enter California without the standard quarantine period. I argued that a presidential horse so carefully bred would be free of disease. This stalling was really political vengeance by officials that did not like the new president. I expressed my frustration to Governor Arturo de la Madrid of Baja California Norte. He assured me that in keeping with his president's orders, he would get the horse across the border in time for Reagan's birthday party in

Santa Barbara. So I washed my hands of the matter.

The governor told me later over margaritas in Mexicali how he carried out his orders: The presidential horse entered the United States as a wetback stallion. The governor in ordinary riding clothes rode the horse bareback into the surf around the border fence at low tide. An assistant in a horse trailer was waiting for him north of the border. The pair trailored the horse, arriving in Santa Barbara as the Reagan birthday party was in full swing.

A Secret Service officer told the ordinary-looking Mexican horseman to let go of the lead rope. He started to walk the stallion across the lawn to the horse-loving Reagan. The clumsy officer yanked on the horse, which was not accustomed to this treatment. The man was pulled off the ground as the horse reared up in front of all the gasping guests. De la Madrid calmly told the officer to let him have the horse. The governor calmed down the beautiful stallion, which he proceeded to walk over to the president-elect. The governor told me that Reagan just laughed off the incident, for he was an experienced horseman himself.

De la Madrid solemnly told me later that both he and President López Portillo just shook their heads upon learning that Reagan had the horse castrated to calm him down. That meant no offspring from this beautiful beast. Old western movies reveal that Reagan was an excellent horseman in his earlier years, but these had gone by. The value of this gift far exceeded the $100 limit for gifts an American official could accept. Who is to complain? The few that know this story won't tell, and a lot of time has passed since then, anyway.

In a few months, I got a polite letter from the Secretary of State stating that my successor had been selected. Since he had wanted me to stay on, he thanked me genuinely for the service I rendered. The staff was dumbfounded with the selection of the next ambassador: former actor John Gavin. The Mexican press was equally surprised and politely annoyed.

The Mexican annoyance stemmed in small part because Gavin's movie career seemed to be over, but mostly because he had lent his name to publicize a Mexican brandy. His handsome face was on billboards all over Mexico. We heard through embassy sources that López Portillo called the brandy owners himself to get rid of the billboards immediately, although the ad contract had a time to run. The owners bluffed with threats of lawsuits, but the president had his way, of course. Within days you could not see a Gavin brandy ad on any billboard in Mexico.

Ambassador Gavin and I got off to a bad start, which took years to overcome. I learned from a Mexican scholar that the leftist Mexican press was going to publish a scholarly article Gavin had written long ago in which he criticized the Mexican *ejido* system of rural cooperatives supported by the government. *Ejidos* were a sacred cow for Mexican revolutionaries, socialists, and communists. This media assault was meant to use Gavin's article to embarrass President-elect Reagan before the two presidents met in El Paso. At a staff meeting we wondered what to do, if anything. It was not a good thing for an incoming ambassador to be the target of such attacks, even if the position he took in the article made sense.

In order to protect the staff who would have to work with Gavin, I took the responsibility for releasing the article to the newspapers before the media assault on Gavin could begin. News stories in Mexico have a life of about two weeks. Any public debate over Gavin's opinions about *ejidos* would be old news before the presidents met. As a courtesy, I wanted Gavin to know that his article would appear and that protecting the president was more important than avoiding embarrassment for him. I could not connect with him by phone, although I left urgent requests at the State Department for him to call back. In the interest of time the article went to press. Our publication took much of the steam out of the attack, Reagan was spared embarrassment, and Gavin never blamed the embassy staff. In his eyes, I was to blame for his embarrassment.

Ambassador Gavin did a good job in Mexico, although he had more trouble with the Mexican press than I did. Gavin knew Mexico, was bilingual, and worked very hard. Later on, I heard that he changed his opinion of me. He must have learned why I did what I did.

Our time in Mexico offered important moments transcending my official role there. The visit we made to Mother's and Dad's hometowns may have been the high points of our stay in Mexico. We were met by cousins by the dozen who turned out to see their relative, *el embajador*. The trip involved a caravan of our family, some staff, and journalists, who thought this was quite newsworthy. Just out of town a bullfight was organized in which boys from Tepetongo ran around the arena, pulling the tails of young charging bulls. Mariachi bands of local boys blasted away, sometimes in tune, as a huge crowd enjoyed a picnic on the riverbank. We suffered through the usual speeches, which noisy children made hard to hear. Mother's hometown of Tepetongo was painted for the occasion, but Dad's hometown of Susticacán took no notice of us. Since the revolution, all our relatives had left Susticacán. A one-day walk from Tepetongo, Susticacán was isolated in a narrow river valley up in the mountains. Although we found no relatives, we saw people who looked like me. I guess that since the 1600s, people had intermarried enough to blend the gene pool. In both towns, I was humbled by the deep pride I could see in the eyes of everyone. Many said they could hardly believe that one of their own was the American ambassador to Mexico.

Both towns became known across Mexico for the first time in view of the television coverage of our visit. One of our cousins in Tepetongo made the best pork sausage I have ever tasted. Everything about his little *chorizo* factory was clean and efficient. I told him that now that Tepetongo was on the map, he should expand production to make more money. He said, "*Primo,* I like things the way they are. Why would I want to sell more than I produce now?" Much the same thing had happened when I met a young Zapotec girl with big black eyes selling pottery on the roadside in Oaxaca. I looked at the beautiful pieces and bought two, even though I knew they would not survive the trip back. I told her that the price could be higher because tourists would just as soon pay more. She looked at me with surprise and calmly said that the clay materials cost nothing, and she knew the time it took to make the pieces. What she was asking for her work was a fair price. Was my materialistic way better than hers and my cousin's? Immigrants from Mexico bring the same values when they work here. I recently hired a Mexican worker to help trim some trees. I think he was undocumented, but as usual, we just don't ask about such things when they need work and we need their labor. The fellow worked hard, and at the end of the day I asked him how much I owed him. He said in Spanish, "Whatever you think is fair." I paid him well, but wondered about his life here, working with values similar to those I found in Tepetongo.

It is curious that many Mexican workers do not think of us as a foreign country. Our side of the border is simply called, *el otro lado,* or the other side. It helps such workers feel at home to encounter so many Spanish-language place names like El Paso, San Diego, Los Angeles, and so forth, all the way up to Colorado and beyond. Spanish-language television and advertising reinforce their Spanish-speaking world and shelter them from having to speak English. When Mexican workers go home, they are somewhat Americanized, taking back new social values as well as their savings.

The embassy staff worked regularly with their Mexican counterparts to help stem the flow of undocumented workers into the United States. The Mexican position was clear in that Mexicans were free to go where they liked and that border controls were our business, not theirs. Besides, both sides understood that Mexico needed the income from their U.S. workers and the resulting reduction of unemployment in Mexico. While we pointed out the double-talk on the Mexican side, they rightly reminded us that these workers would not cross the border at great cost and personal risk, if they were not sure that Americans would hire them. Indeed, major U.S. industries depended on undocumented Mexican workers, especially farmers, even if employing these workers was illegal. César Chávez, the great leader of American farmworkers, refused for years to visit Mexico or talk to Mexican officials in view of the refusal of the Mexican government to stop undocumented workers from flooding the farm labor market in the United States.

Part of the Mexican double-talk on immigration was evident in that Mexico gave very few work permits to American citizens. Even Mexican firms that wanted to hire an American specialist to help get them started had little success in obtaining a work permit for an American. Quite a bit of my time was spent trying to talk a charming Mexican official into approving work permit applications, even when these workers would be valuable to the Mexican economy. This lady reflected the official policy of anti-Americanism in this area. In some notable cases, factory construction was held up while a Mexican firm waited months for a work permit for an American specialist. I had to swallow my pride each time I called this lady, who enjoyed giving an

American ambassador a hard time. Such calls were normally made by a staff member, but I tried to break the bottleneck, with little success. I once said to her in polite frustration that I probably could not get a work permit to join a Mexican university, and she agreed. Since her superiors were the origin of her conduct, I went to the public media. I said to the press that more Mexican politicians should read American history and learn how immigration has made us strong. Indeed, even undocumented Mexican farmworkers make us wealthier.

Later, during the presidency of Carlos Salinas de Gortari, César Chávez and the president finally met in Los Angeles. I was there during the talks that led to providing Mexican workers in the United States with credits for Social Security benefits when the workers returned to Mexico. Mexico and César Chávez finally reached an understanding on this part of the problem.

At the meeting in Los Angeles, President Salinas asked several Mexican-American leaders to make brief statements to him and the advisors accompanying him about U.S.-Mexican relations. I was among ten speaking for five minutes each. The harmful effects of undocumented workers on barrio employment was on everyone's mind, so I discussed other matters. Eyebrows went up when I stated that there was no justification for poverty in Mexico, except that certain powerful groups profited from poverty. One need only look at little Japan to imagine how rich Mexico could be, with its natural resources, climate, and proximity to the world's largest consumer market. Mexico would be dumb if it continued restricting American imports and put off selling all it could to us. I used the word *pendejos,* which is a strong word for dumb in Spanish. The president just looked right at me and then over to advisors on each side with a meaningful glance, as if to say "You see!"

It is probably a coincidence in timing, but some months later Carlos Salinas de Gortari made the historic suggestion for what came to be called NAFTA, the North American Free Trade Association. By 1980, Mexican scholars were claiming that Mexico was losing some of its best people to the United States by immigration documented and undocumented. This "brain drain" could be stopped by expanding opportunities in Mexico for both Mexican laborers and professionals. For my part, I stated in talks here and in Mexico that continued undocumented immigration would soon cause a general reaction in the United States. Such measures against Mexican immigration might not be fair or wise.

President Carter was more right than he guessed when he appointed me as ambassador to Mexico. I chose to speak out on troublesome issues, such as immigration and drugs, to influential groups of all sorts in Mexico. Many did not like to hear what I said, but no one ever claimed that I was mistaken when I blamed powerful economic groups in Mexico for the lack of jobs that drove surplus workers to leave their homes. Mexicans commonly blame the United States for their economic conditions, and I would contradict this whenever I could by giving examples of how poverty in Mexico was part of the Mexican political system. I observed that it was easier to control a poor population in the short term, but that long-range prosperity for all was being sacrificed.

Within the United States, the trend among white, non-Hispanic Americans was to reduce the number of their children. This reduction in the average family size of the American population was producing a situation in which maintaining the proportion of white population to the whole was in question. The decline in the size of the average American family is evident in our own, for that part. My parents had eight children, while Pat and I had only three. Also, employment patterns and social changes in the United States explain why Mexican workers are necessary to do farm labor and other manual jobs that Americans are no longer willing to do. Just the same, I observed in talks to Mexican groups that anti-immigrant feelings were going to be contrary to U.S. economic interests. If unemployed Americans were willing to do the same work done by undocumented Mexican workers, we would not need these folks, and they would not come.

My predictions of punitive measures against immigration came about at the federal and state levels within ten years. Anti-immigrant feelings are not new in our country. Looking back, one can trace anti-immigrant sentiment over the two hundred years of our history. The Germans, Irish, Southern Europeans, Asians, and others had suffered from periods of anti-immigrant sentiment since the 1830s, and now it was the Mexicans' turn. Whether or not they were an asset to the United States, a new form of nativism targeted them as less American and a threat to society. All the while, even public opponents of immigration took advantage of lower-cost Mexican workers. Even members of presidential cabinets and Governor Pete Wilson in California, who opposed Mexican immigration, hired Mexican domestic help.

Governor Pete Wilson championed eliminating all public health and educational benefits to undocumented residents and even to legal alien residents on the road to citizenship. It is probably a coincidence that I suggested to a prominent attorney and strong supporter of Governor Wilson that, should newly elected Governor Wilson decide to run for president, he would make a name for himself by opposing affirmative action programs as well. Before long, Wilson broke his promise to remain as governor and became famous nationally by calling for an end to affirmative action. This former U.S. marine was now saying things about immigration publicly that millions were thinking privately.

I had reasons for appearing to help Governor Wilson that Machiavelli would have applauded. The new preferences for minorities, including women, were entrenched in federal and state laws since the presidency of Lyndon Baines Johnson. As minorities grew in numbers and displaced equally qualified white people in some jobs, opposition swelled against this form of special treatment for minorities. Since the presidency of Johnson, minorities, women, the poor, and the undereducated were gaining help as never before. Although "empowerment" of the poor and disadvantaged was admirable, groups who had enjoyed power now feared a loss of their privileges. I recall that within the Department of History at my university, the majority of the male faculty refused to rehire a female colleague in order to maintain the male composition of the department. One of her major problems was that she was vocal and energetic in her opinions. She was a threat to insecure male egos. White Anglo-American women needed affirmation action no less than minority groups and were to suffer when it was terminated. Hypocrisy was common regarding affirmative Action. Banks, corporations, agribusiness, and other powerful groups had long enjoyed special treatment from governmental agencies and federal tax laws.

In appearing to help Governor Wilson, I bore in mind that Mexican Americans gained far less than American blacks from affirmative action. Indeed, most blacks took affirmative action as something meant for their benefit and shoved aside the efforts of Mexican Americans to share in the benefits of these programs. I was personally the victim of black racism against Mexican Americans in my own career. Blacks promoted the political attitude that whites in America today owed blacks a debt for slavery and discrimination in the past. This attitude was supported by guilt-ridden whites, who were afraid to oppose black demands.

Mexican Americans would have to wait in line until blacks were paid back for this sorry history. Both political parties accepted this position.

I was among the Mexican-American leaders who voiced ever stronger resentment of this treatment and argued that we should be allies, not competitors. Only until Mexican Americans voted in numbers that corresponded to their population could such conditions change. How could we increase voter turnout? In the 1980s, only about 20 percent of Mexican-American qualified voters went to the polls. The voter turnout was greater in some parts of Texas and New Mexico, but the group was largely powerless, compared to blacks who mobilized about 75 percent of their qualified voter population.

I believed that we had to be victimized in a very clear manner that would awaken what was commonly known as the Hispanic "sleeping giant." Governor Wilson could be led into helping wake up this voting bloc. It was at a Pomona College Trustees meeting that I jokingly gave a Republican friend the tip for Governor Pete Wilson's rumored presidential race. I could only wonder whether he would pass along that insight. Wilson's presidential bid ran out of steam quickly, but he did emerge as the major national figure opposing affirmative action and the champion against the Mexican invasion.

Governor Wilson claimed these Mexican "illegals" were living off welfare programs and overloading our schools. He pictured thousands of pregnant Mexican girls sneaking across the line to give birth to Americans on our side of the border. Many studies were done as to whether these folks paid their own way through taxes or were a burden to other taxpayers. The scholarly judgment emerged that undocumented workers more than paid for any public benefits that some of them received. This curious situation emerged because most of these immigrant workers did not approach public agencies for fear of being deported, although they unavoidably paid taxes that provided the agency services.

I felt very strongly about this dilemma because I have never forgotten that the Nava family was to be pushed out during an earlier episode of anti-Mexican feelings. Our parents were legal resident aliens, but their eight children were native-born Americans. Too young to stay here alone, the children were going to Mexico with their parents, until my sudden surgery stopped their repatriation. Even if our own country was throwing us out, before long, three of the four sons put on uniforms to serve our country. Carlos was too old to serve, or else he would have joined the service also. After all, we were Americans, not Mexicans.

During my service in Mexico, I assumed that President Carter would be reelected in 1980. However, Carter lost overwhelmingly to Ronald Reagan, former movie actor and governor of California. Although presidents tended to be reelected, poor Carter did not stand a chance, due to circumstances beyond his control, such as the hostages taken in Iran and the poor economic conditions at home. Many leaders in the Democratic Party sat on their hands and did little to help Carter. Others, such as Senator Ted Kennedy, openly revolted. Kennedy announced that he would run for the Democratic Party nomination for president. Indeed, I would never have been appointed were it not for the fact that my predecessor, Patrick Lucey, resigned to support Senator Kennedy in his run against the man who had honored him with such a position.

I talked with Lucey in Washington, D.C. before leaving for Mexico City to get his insights on the situation there. He said little, however, and radiated embarrassment. I shared his embarrassment, but wanted to know whatever he had to say about relations with Mexico. Senator Kennedy withdrew his candidacy for president, but his challenge did much damage to "the boss," as we referred to Carter. Lucey did confess to one frustrating failure while in Mexico. In spite of tutors, he could not learn Spanish and was forced to rely on translators.

I was worried about Carter's reelection in view of information available at the embassy. Carter's loss was largely the product of the Arab oil embargo (and a resulting global economic downturn), which he had inherited. People in public office are quick to take the credit for favorable developments they did not bring about. The public gives credit when it is not deserved, but the public also blames an officeholder when things get bad, whether or not it's his fault. The economic recession was not the only handicap Carter faced.

What caused the most damage to Carter was the humiliation we suffered when young people in Iran seized the American embassy and staff in Tehran. The seizure of a foreign embassy is very rare because it is considered something beyond the bounds of civilized relations between nations. President Carter was blamed by the average voter because he failed to recover the embassy and American hostages. Even a military rescue mission had failed, bringing shame on our military power.

Secretary of State Edmund Muskie and his wife visited us in Mexico during the presidential campaign. We hosted them in the spacious residence and shared meals like a family. The last supper was a disaster, however. When the Muskies left for Washington, our relationship was torn apart. I was in low esteem with my boss.

During supper, the American response to the hostage crisis came up for discussion. At that time, Carmen and Katie read every book they could get their hands on. They were actively involved in the discussion, when Katie inquired about the rumors that President Carter might pay ransom for release of the hostages. Muskie got red in the face and blew up. He shouted that the rumors were false. President Carter had not offered to ransom the hostages. He went on for some time while everyone at the elegant table and the servants just looked at him in amazement. Like the others, I just sat there and listened to him with amazement, but I wondered if there was justification for him to react so defensively. Was there substance to the rumors? If so, he would be intimately involved as Secretary of State.

I was so proud of Katie. Rather than shrink away at the attack by her father's boss, she calmly pursued her remarks when he stopped. Mrs. Muskie cut in and managed to change the subject after she credited the girls for their unusual knowledge at their age about foreign affairs.

Early the next morning, the staff tipped me off that the Secretary of State had secretly moved ahead his departure for Washington. Except for the loyalty of my staff, I would have failed to bid farewell to the Secretary of State at a remote and secure part of the Mexico City airport. I dreaded the idea that Muskie might tell President Carter that his ambassador in Mexico failed to see him off at the airport. Muskie was surprised to see me waiting for him at the isolated airport ramp, along with my embassy troops and high Mexican officials. I took special delight in bidding him farewell in glowing words that made it clear that I meant the opposite of what I was saying. This technique is very Mexican, by the way. Muskie had demonstrated an inability to control his emotions in public life before, but how dare he scold Katie at our dinner table!

I figured that Carter might offer to pay ransom for the release of the hostages after the use of military force had failed shamefully. A special American military unit had tried to drop into Tehran by helicopter only to abort the rescue when two of the ships collided at takeoff from a sandy desert staging ground, killing numerous U.S. troops. The United States was embarrassed by the negative global reaction.

The president asked ambassadors for their insights, so I sent in my recommendations for rescuing the hostages, but I will never know if these got past the State Department. I urged that in keeping with the Islamic law guiding the avowedly religious regime of Iran, the United States express formal regrets for its unjust actions against that nation in the past. If the United States publicly acknowledged our past disgraceful acts, and promised to not do such things again, and offered to make amends, then by Islamic law, the Iranian government would find just cause to release the hostages. Both government officials knew that years before, we had organized the overthrow of Iran's popularly elected Mohammed Mossadegh and consented to his execution in a plot financed by our CIA These were the actions that explained Iranian hatred for us and contributed to the seizure of our embassy.

Admission of American wrongdoing to Iran had the best chance of gaining release of our hostages, I believed. In addition to engineering the disposal of Mohammed Mossadegh, the United States had further wronged the Iranians by installing the dictatorial Shah Mohammed Reza Pahlavi. Our foreign policy in this region was dominated by the interests of European and American petroleum companies. These interests feared popular rule in Iran. When the shah was forced to abdicate his throne years later, a religious leader in French exile returned to gain control over all aspects of Iranian life. The Ayatollah Khomeini enjoyed complete power and hated the United States. However, President Carter had to deal with him. Since everything else had failed, why not use the Ayatollah's religious faith to gain our ends? I guessed beforehand that apologies by great powers are rare, even when called for. Anyway, I tried.

As it turned out, the Reagan presidential campaign was deathly afraid of an "October surprise," that is, a successful rescue of the hostages so late in the campaign as to make President Carter a hero and leave little time for the Reagan campaign to stage a political counterattack before the first Tuesday of November 1980. For reasons that still escape me, the American public does not understand that the Reagan campaign bribed the Iranian government not to release the hostages until after Reagan's election to the presidency. I figured that political leaders who knew what happened were so embarrassed at what the Reagan election team had done that they worked hard to hide the full facts from the American public.

With the Iranians delaying the release of the American hostages until Reagan was elected, each side would obtain their own goals: Reagan would get elected, and then the new administration would sell Iran weapons that it desperately needed against the neighboring country of Iraq, which had recently invaded Iran. At this time, the United States supported the Iraqi dictator, Saddam Hussein, even though he had invaded Iran and used poisonous gas there.

The plan called for Israel to be the supplier of the American weapons sold to Iran in return for the release of our hostages. The arrangements for the secret sale of the weapons to Iran were made during a highly secret meeting in Europe late in the presidential campaign. George Bush was Reagan's vice presidential candidate. Bush had also been director of the CIA, and although he denied taking part in these negotiations, knowledgeable people were convinced that he had simply covered his tracks completely. The CIA can fool our detection network and fly airplanes in and out of countries undetected, I had been informed as part of my briefing.

The day that Ronald Reagan took the oath of office in Washington, events took place that support what I have said. The American hostages, now well fed and recovered from their year's ordeal, were flown to a secret base in Germany. They looked just fine in new clothes. As they came down the plane's ramp six hours ahead of Washington, D.C. time, President Carter greeted them warmly one by one. It had taken time to make all these preparations, lending weight to the conclusion that the arrangement had been made some time before.

This shabby and secret scheme stole the presidency, in my view. The media must have understood the implications of what happened, but either could not believe it or chose not to embarrass the incoming president. Presidents Reagan and Bush came to dominate the American public media almost as much as administrations do in Mexico, as later events demonstrated.

The boomerang swung back after the theft of the presidency, striking the schemers and the nation as well. Employees of the CIA, the president's staff, and a gang of semi-independent operators, in keeping with the secret deal, sold weapons to Iran at inflated prices. They profited personally and used the rest to support the conservative Contra rebels fighting against the communist regime in Nicaragua. This support was against a law enacted by Congress under President Carter specifically to rule out American involvement in troubled Nicaraguan affairs. At this time, Carter and many Americans believed that it was possible to work with the youthful Marxist leaders in Nicaragua who had overthrown one of the Americas' worst dictators. Many Americans believed that the Sandinista regime in Nicaragua could be persuaded to use democratic political procedures. As it turned out, the Sandinista regime did submit to free elections and lost peacefully.

The Iran-Contra scandal burst out when an Arab middleman spilled the beans to a newspaper in Lebanon, claiming that he was cheated out of his fees for helping in this business. President Reagan and Vice President Bush at first denied these sales took place and then claimed they knew nothing about them, even though American planes were used for transportation. For a while this scandal looked like the Watergate scandal that had forced President Richard Nixon to resign. Reagan survived the Iran-Contra scandal because the Senate committee simply refused to make public the testimony that would have doomed the presidency. Vice President Bush went on to get elected president after two terms of President Reagan. In my view, the historical reputation of President Carter will outlive and outshine those of Reagan and Bush, even if these two had their way at the time.

When I met president-elect Reagan in El Paso to confer with Mexican president López Portillo, we had a curious exchange. Reagan probably knew about me since his days as California governor because I was on the school board and often spoke publicly. Since public education was nonpartisan, we had common friends. In any case, following our discussion with the Mexican president, I asked to speak privately with Reagan, and we shared a cordial conversation as he got ready to board a special airplane. I simply told him that I would be happy to stay on and would do the job he wanted faithfully. He mentioned hearing that members of the U.S. Chamber of Commerce had written, asking that I be kept on, but he was noncommittal. With his appointment of John Gavin to replace me, it became obvious that, in fact, Reagan had other plans.

I was very sorry to leave the post. By now, the Mexican print and television media were helping me interpret the United States to the Mexican public as no previous American ambassador had done. American ambassadors before me had been wealthy businessmen with little firsthand knowledge of Mexico or its troubled history with the United States. I had taken time to meet with individuals from all walks of life. Now and then I purposely asked my driver/guard to stop at random to have some enchiladas or tacos at a sidewalk stand. What expressions of surprise greeted me in the faces of passersby. Mexican news reports about this gradually began to change the image of a U.S. ambassador, and of the United States as well.

On the other hand, Pat and I found consolation in that the children would be less likely to become spoiled by all the special attention they got. The children escaped the dangers of public office because we kept reminding them that all the ceremony and attention was temporary and make-believe. All this would pass, we said, and we would all return to our home in Northridge, where I would mow the lawn again and wash the cars, while Pat would care for us again without the help of numerous servants. Keeping a hold on reality took special effort in light of all the special attention lavished on us. In one case, the chief of police flew the girls home in his helicopter after a volleyball game at their school so they could attend a reception at the residence. How do you keep a hold on real life after that sort of treatment?

There were many things to do before we left. No specific deadline was set, and so we made the visits to other ambassadors required by protocol and personal obligations to friends. The best thing about the gesture of visits was that all the ambassadors in Mexico had their signature engraved in a beautiful silver serving tray as a parting gift to us. Whenever we use it, we are reminded of that fairy-tale experience when we represented the president of the United States.

One interesting episode occurred during the closing of my office. Some of my working papers were stamped confidential or classified, and others were borderline in their sensitivity. All were historical materials, however. I asked for advice from the security officer. This chap reviewed my office after I left every day to make certain that I had not left any sensitive materials on my desk by mistake. The cleaning crew was all Mexican and most reliable on security matters, but we made double sure just in case. When I asked the security officer who placed the office files into the categories of sensitivity, he looked surprised and just said, "Why, you do, sir."

It took days to review my office papers, and I fudged in the direction of historical records by packing up some very interesting photos, letters, reports, and files. These are now in the archives of the university for researchers to use. While the file cabinet of ambassadorial papers was still in my campus office for graduate students to use, an interesting Hispanic fellow came by and said that the Ronald Reagan Presidential Library in the Simi Valley nearby might want to house these papers, since the end of my service was under President Reagan. I purposely left him alone the following week to look through them, but left some discrete markers on a few choice pieces. After his review, he thanked me kindly and stated the library would be in touch with me, but they never called. Looking through the files, I noticed that a few pieces I had marked were missing. So, although I brought home just about everything I wanted, the FBI or CIA took what it wanted. I can sleep peacefully because I had made xerox copies of the choice items before the "Reagan Library" fellow lifted some without telling me. The ambassadorial papers are in the university library for public access.

Chapter 25

Back in California

Our home in Northridge was just as we had left it. My sister Rosemarie and her husband, Charles, had moved into it while we were gone. They just closed down their home and lived in ours. Everything was already in place when we returned.

Just before I left Mexico, a member of the California State University Board of Trustees called to invite my application for the presidency of the California State University at Fullerton. He thought I had a great chance for the position, coming after the position of ambassador. A black woman was selected instead. After losing out to a black fellow for the presidency at California State University in Los Angeles just before the ambassadorship, a black fellow for the California State Community College Chancellorship, and some Anglo fellow for the job at California State University Fresno, the disappointment with Fullerton made me lose heart in the system to which I had dedicated my career. This final disappointment led me to retire.

I wanted to do some new things related to teaching, and so I signed up for an early retirement plan. Teaching during the fall semester only, I would be free between New Year's and Labor Day each year. The early retirement program would give me a lot of free time and the prospects of making up for the loss of one half of my regular income through new and interesting projects. At least, that's what I figured. I was driven to retire more by pride than good sense, however. The income did not materialize, although the interesting projects did.

We soon adjusted to not being important people anymore. The main link to our former life was the occasional call from American newspapers or television reporters for remarks on U.S. and Mexican relations, but these gradually dropped in frequency. Oddly enough, Mexican reporters both locally and from Mexico City called about bilateral issues for years afterward, and still do.

Chapter 26

Building Our Dream House in the Mountains

Building a home near Big Bear Lake was the first big project upon our return from Mexico. For two years we had paid for the parcel and spent many a breakfast at Joyce's Coffee Shop in Northridge, where we drew plans on the paper place mats. The house in tall pines would look down the valley toward Baldwin Lake. Pat's brother and wife were building on their parcel bordering to the east, so we figured that we could enjoy life close to each other.

The first thing we did was to have a water well dug and electric power brought in underground to preserve the view. All of a sudden, the shop courses I was pushed into in public schools and the experiences earning my way through college came in very handy. The logs came from southwestern Colorado. Pat spotted them as we drove home in our house trailer from Colorado Springs. Pat saw a family mill cutting logs as we drove by, and we came to a screeching halt. The millers calculated the number of logs from the floor plan, and before long a huge truck hauled them up to 7,000 feet in the San Bernardino Mountains, where the foundation waited for them.

I taught Carmen, Katie, and Paul how to use the power and hand equipment so they would be self-sufficent in this sort of thing. We built the huge barn first in order to store supplies and set up the table saws, drills, and other equipment. As a first-rate builder, Uncle Larry and a contractor friend guided us and did the complicated things. We did the grunt work, and after the roof was set in place just before snow fell, we started to do all the indoor finishing. The kitchen tile work is our pride and joy. Pat ordered hand-painted tile from Valencia, Spain. A handbook on tile setting guided us, and the work looks professional. All the house is somewhat rustic, as we planned, but the rugs are authentic Persians and the stereo equipment is first-rate. We still refuse to put in a television.

During the time we were finishing the home in Big Bear, I got involved in a curious project with *charro* friends. We exchanged news while sitting on our horses and enjoying cold beers one day. I brought up my mother's hometown, which was now getting its first secondary school. Federal funds had run out mysteriously, and the children would have to sit on the floor, which gets very cold in winter in the mountains of Zacatecas. One of the fellows said in Spanish, "To hell with the corrupt government. Let's build the desks and drive them down in our horse trailers."

Before long, we were building several hundred desks and benches in our garages. Our garage and that of our cousin Miguel Flores were the focal points of the project. One of the fellows was especially good at carpentry, so he made a design that permitted cutting, drilling, and finishing the furniture in pieces that could be stacked in a four-horse trailer. The pieces could then be assembled in Tepetongo. The pieces weighed no more than four horses.

Our nephew Andrew Hernández took his motor home, in which we ate on the long drive. At the border in El Paso, the customs official tried to extort money from us, even though we had letters from the school principal and mayor that the shipment was destined for a public school and not for sale. We reached an impasse with the official and dreaded returning to Los Angeles with the desks. I politely asked for the use of the corrupt man's telephone. When he obliged, I called Mexico City and asked to speak to the minister of the interior, who by luck took the call. This fat little Caesar could not believe whom I was speaking to. The minister asked to speak to fatso, who started to sweat with apologies. He escorted our caravan all the way out of town and promised to phone ahead to make sure we had no problem at other road checks where Mexicans going home suffer extortion.

We met with the governor of Zacatecas on the way to Tepetongo. We suggested a formal program to promote cooperation between Mexican hometowns and their immigrants in the United States. He was fascinated with the idea and promised support. In Tepetongo, high school students helped us assemble the desks and benches. Everyone we spoke to agreed that people-to-people projects were better than sending money to the local government because local politicians tended to steal the money, like the customs official. By now, hundreds of such projects have eclipsed this modest one in 1981. The latest figures count about $400 million raised annually in the United States by Zacatecans for their hometowns.

Recently, the three candidates for governor of the leading national political party, PRI, debated before Zacatecans in East Los Angeles. The governorship of Zacatecas went to another party, the PRD. The PRI party that has dominated Mexican politics for more than sixty-five years was wounded. Since more Zacatecans now live in the United States than in Zacatecas, campaigning here seems to make sense. Ricardo Monreal, the successful candidate for governor, had a political rally at our home. A unique event, I understand. Other Mexican states probably will follow the

Zacatecas example. Cross-border life is beginning to be rather curious.

Vicente Fox, Mexico's new president in 2000, made it clear that he will draw closer at the presidential level with the millions of Mexicans living in the United States. Other Americans will look harder at the closer relationship between Mexican clubs and associations and official Mexican agencies. Closely linked to this development is the ability of Mexican Americans like me to apply for dual citizenship, as long as at least one parent was born in Mexico. Without violating the essential elements of U.S. citizenship, Mexican Americans will be able to enjoy some benefits of Mexican citizenship, such as property ownership and residence.

Chapter 27

Producing a Documentary and Reflecting on Communist Cuba

My first visit to Cuba took place right after the dictator Fulgencio Batista fled Havana in December 1959. A mass uprising overthrew his corrupt government, and almost everyone in the United States welcomed the change. I flew down just as the revolutionary government was taking over. There was still a lot of disorder and confusion. I would not do such a thing now. I was a single professor of history and could afford to take such chances in search of adventure and firsthand information.

I went to Cuba feeling sympathetic for the revolution. However, I returned to Los Angeles critical of the Cuban Revolution and spoke out against it several times. I still have a tape recording of a major debate in Hollywood with the Fair Play for Cuba Committee. I argued that it was good that Cuban and American gangsters were driven out along with the corrupt police. However, I did not approve of the governmental seizure of newspapers and radio and television stations on the island. Since all of the supporters of the corrupt dictator had fled with him, why was it necessary to seize control of all the news media?

Since I looked and dressed like a native, I went to many places and listened to people who thought I was Mexican because of my speech. Everyone supported the revolution.

I recall one evening speech by Fidel Castro in a huge plaza with about half a million people cheering his every word. He spoke endlessly, so after three hours of standing, I gave up and went back to my cheap hotel room. I noticed by chance that my belongings were not placed in my suitcase as I had packed them. The next day I rearranged everything in a particular manner and pasted one of my hairs on the side of the suitcase with saliva. Sure enough, at the end of the day the hair was gone, and the belongings were arranged almost as I had left them. I took the first plane out of Havana the next morning and was greatly relieved when the airliner left the ground and swung north toward Miami.

I remembered my first visit in 1960 as the airliner approached José Martí Airport in 1993. The runway was lined with Russian aircraft as we rolled to a stop. I was sweaty because it was not only hot but I wondered whether my senior travel companion, Ernesto Vera, would be there to greet me. What if he was not there? Pat and the children relied on my judgment, but I could tell they were worried about my trip to Cuba.

One night, over some Basque food and wine back in Pamplona, Spain, Ernesto Vera and I started talking about Cuba, which was in the news. From one moment to the next we jumped into the car and drove to Madrid, where we met with officials of the Cuban embassy and proposed a film documentary on Cuba. We took their advice and prepared a long proposal, which was faxed to Havana. Officials in Cuba approved the project in principle a few months later. The officials insisted on talking personally in Havana before final permission to film might be given. Ernesto flew in from Spain, and I sneaked into Cuba through Mexico because it was very difficult to get permission from the U.S. government to visit Cuba.

Ernesto and I assumed that our room in the Riviera Hotel

was bugged, so we spoke bearing that in mind. The officials in the international press office liked the proposal, even though they knew about my opposition to the communist system there. As one official put it, "We know about your academic and diplomatic career as well as your positions on Cuba, but you have always been fair and well-informed. We are not afraid of what you will produce." This attitude reflected Cuban confidence in their system, it seemed to me. We left after a week, each to his own country, in order to raise production money.

The money for the Cuban filming appeared in the most unexpected way. A cousin, Steve Muñatones, introduced me to a client from Hawaii, who needed ideas for creating a nonprofit foundation in the islands. The two flew in from the islands for a supper. At the end of our talk, Dwyane asked me what I was doing these days, and I told him about the plans for a documentary film on Cuba. As a multimillionaire businessman, he asked why I would do a documentary on a communist country. I explained that it was in the interest of the American public to know more about Cuba. He understood because he was born into a very poor Japanese family on the islands. They had suffered at the hands of white Americans in ways the Navas had. He sympathized with Cubans who have been dominated by the United States since 1898. Out of the clear blue sky, he asked me how much money I needed to complete the job. I never expected such a question! I took time to sip some coffee as my mind went through all the things needed to give him a figure. I said $80,000 would do the job, given work that had been done already. "Fine," he said, "the money will go to your bank number as soon as you fax it to me."

My daughter Carmen confessed to some anxiety about having her husband, Todd, go to Cuba with us. She feared that both her husband and dad would land in a Cuban jail, but confidence in her dad overcame most of her fears. Todd and I began to make plans for the filming right away. Only after we had returned safely did Todd confess that he also had shared some of Carmen's anxieties.

As the plane landed in Havana, Todd was very excited because he had never before gone on such an adventure. To save production money, his childhood friend, Larry Sterling, came along as second cameraman. He closed down his photographic studio in order to go with his pal on this wild adventure. Larry's wife was on the verge of tears as she took numerous pictures when the three of us drove off for the airport. We looked back and she was clutching their baby. Larry had never been farther from home than Tijuana, and later, his eyes were bigger than Todd's as we went through Cuban customs.

Ernesto Vera and Carlos Arbillo were in Havana to greet us. They had come earlier from Spain in order to line up people and places to shoot. This advance work made it possible to get all the filming done quickly. We went from one place or person to another, like clockwork. The Cuban film crew was wonderful. They worked for next to nothing, and so we gave them a very generous bonus when we left the island two weeks later.

Relations between Cuba and our country are fascinating. Below is one of my newspaper editorials on the subject. The Los Angeles newspaper gave it almost a full page, alongside a photograph of Castro.

Embargo just serves to impede reforms in Cuba
Los Angeles Daily News, Sunday, July 27, 1997
by
Julian Nava

It may surprise many to hear that Fidel Castro is

himself our best ally for bringing about changes in Cuba in the direction we have sought for so long. After all, "constructive engagement" with the Soviet Union, Communist China, Vietnam, and now even North Korea has been supported by both American parties as the most productive policy to open up these communist societies. The American news media still suffer from a Cold War frame of mind, and therefore, the American public hears little about the positive changes under way in Cuba, which only Castro could bring about. Over the opposition of communist hard-liners, Cubans can now possess and do business in dollars. More than 135 private businesses now operate in a market-like manner, while investors from scores of countries now invest in Cuba again. Cubans seek American professors to teach them how to operate businesses in the global marketplace Cuba is joining in spite of our American embargo. Fidel Castro has read the handwriting on the wall. Have we?

The introduction in Congress of the Cuban Humanitarian Trade Act of 1997 will provoke a lively and enlightening debate over basic American principles that we assume guide our foreign policy. This act would exempt from the 37-year trade embargo against Cuba, commerce in medicines and food with the island. As more Americans visit Cuba and various domestic and international agencies study Cuban living conditions, the American denial of food and medical materials appears as cruelty against innocent people that is unworthy of our American principles.

Bill Clinton is the ninth American president who has maintained the embargo designed to punish the Cuban public until it overthrows the communist regime. Clinton has greatly tightened the embargo by signing into law the Helms-Burton Act early in 1996. By threatening foreigners who traffic in Cuban properties formerly owned by Cuban exiles, Clinton incurred the wrath of the world. Clinton made a far more serious mistake, however. He codified the U.S. embargo. That is, he made it federal law. Now, any changes in the embargo must originate in Congress. He gave up the precious constitutional prerogative of the president to make foreign policy. As matters stand now in our relations with Cuba, a single committee chairman, like Jesse Helms, can bottle up any changes in U.S.-Cuban policy.

How did we get to this point since the dictator, Fulgencio Batista, fled Cuba in 1959 in the face of a mass public uprising? Batista was openly a tool of American special interests whose army was U.S. trained and supplied. The American mob controlled the tourist industry along with organized crime in Cuba. In light of our domination of Cuba since its independence from Spain in 1898, the United States was an ideal enemy to energize revolutionary passions and justify the socialist reforms.

President Eisenhower tried to reach an understanding with a young Fidel Castro, as he did with anti-Russian communist Marshal Tito in Yugoslavia. As Castro proceeded to seize the properties of corrupt Batista officials and the American mob, even Americans applauded. When expropriations of American companies followed, Eisenhower drew a line and started the embargo on a modest scale, still hoping for the best. As the Soviets quickly offered to buy anything the United States boycotted, the Cuban-Soviet alliance was born.

The first generation of Cuban exiles included not only good people who were now fearful of the revolution, but a large number of American and Cuban gangsters with a tradition of violence and unscrupulous conduct. These still seek bloody revenge and contribute generously to American congressmen who do their bidding. Leaders among the anti-Castro exiles are the authors of the Helms-Burton Act.

Recent CIA disclosures have now revealed a policy denied for over 30 years. The CIA paid for efforts by Cuban exiles and the Mafia to assassinate Castro, not always with the knowledge of the current American president. The disclosures point to 11 attempts, while Castro proudly claims 12. However, we cannot escape the consequences of this disreputable conduct in shaping the Cuban official attitude towards us. To his credit, President Carter ended all attempts to assassinate foreign chiefs of state on both practical grounds as well as principle.

One school of thought has claimed Cubans were involved in the Kennedy assassination and that this dastardly act justifies our enmity towards the entire Cuban population. We can wonder which Cubans may have been involved—Castro agents or Cuban exiles who have never forgiven Kennedy for dooming the Bay of Pigs invasion of Cuba in 1961 by denying U.S. air support. The duplicity of our government at times knows few bounds. Grudgingly, the American public was told that U.S. Army personnel trained Cuban exiles in Central America only. Recently I talked to two American officers who trained Cuban exiles for the Bay of Pigs invasion in Fort Ord, California. In Cuban eyes, that constituted an American invasion. American hostility towards Cuba stems from other sources not revealed to the American public. I spoke to a Cuban military officer who proudly related how Cuba diverted Cuban-bound Soviet ground-to-air missiles to the Viet Cong. As the U.S. lost control of the skies, even our diehards realized the war was unwinnable. This Cuban fellow who trained the Viet Cong to use the missiles said, "Americans should thank us for saving lives by shortening that stupid war." The Pentagon has not forgotten this Cuban involvement nor forgiven it after all these years.

During my filming of a recent documentary in Cuba, an older lady blurted out a clue to a more effective and honorable American policy towards Cuba. I asked her what would happen if Castro suddenly died. She replied in a shout, "God forbid it! Fidel is the only one who can proceed with the changes in the system which he has started." She went on to say that Cuba now trades in dollars as well as pesos. Castro is systematically replacing the old guard with young men and women in the highest posts. While it may seem audacious to see Castro as providing a transition to an open society, that is precisely the new role he has set for himself despite the opposition from communist hard-liners. A high level Cuban confessed after a few drinks I bought for him, "You Americans are stupid. After all these years, you do not understand us. If you were to restore normal relations—you know, trade, tourism, and education—we would get voted out in the next elections. Your hostility keeps the party in power."

Cubans share our culture and pose no threat to us. Granted, some special interests in the U.S. fear the spread to Latin America of Cuban social gains, such as Social Security, free medical coverage, and education at all levels. A lion trainer in Havana said to me, "Since you guys claim all this is a mess, take away the embargo, and let us see how much of a mess it is."

Chapter 28

MEXICAN *EJIDOS*

Our relations with Mexico are largely shaped by economic forces. A major force shaping bilateral relations is the poverty of most Mexicans, especially the farmers. Among the poorest farmers are the families that live on *ejidos,* or rural cooperatives.

My good friend Professor Jerry Straughan and his wife Susanna got me involved in helping cooperatives in Baja California while I was on the school board, and the activity has continued down to the present. During the term of leftist President Luis Echeverría, millions of acres of land were given to groups of Mexican families, pretty much like our homestead grant program during the nineteenth century. The land grants to these groups totaled more than half of the entire peninsula. The long peninsula was almost vacant then and still is. However, it holds vast mineral resources, farmlands, and endless beautiful beaches. Most of these *ejido* groups were disadvantaged because they lacked education and technical skills to develop their vast holdings. Just as important, they lacked capital.

Jerry had a project under way to help one *ejido* develop Mexico's first oyster-growing farm on the coast of Baja, about 70 miles south of Ensenada in a bay called Bahía Falsa. Before long, Jerry and I were picking up frozen oyster eggs from Washington state at the Los Angeles airport. We would race down the coast with the eggs packed in dry ice to where *ejido* workers placed the eggs in special saltwater tanks for early development before they would be put out in the shallow bay for maturation into oysters. Jerry had recruited American specialists to train the *ejido* fellows in this process. This installation came to be Mexico's first oyster farm and soon convinced the government that oyster growing could be a major industry. In all this activity that went on for several years, Jerry and I always gave full credit to the Mexican *ejido* in order to avoid charges that Americans were interfering in the internal economic affairs of Mexico. More important was the need to build self-confidence among the *ejido* owners. They needed self-confidence more than money.

After this success, we decided to enter an activity that would produce income for us for a change. The new project was a wonderful idea in every respect, and yet it failed in every respect.

In alliance with a prosperous company of winter crop farmers here in California, we shaped a company to gather *ejido* farmers in the northern Sea of Cortez into a unique organization. Pooling their valuable land and water rights to the Colorado River, they could grow winter crops for the Southern California market. The prospects were enormous because our main Mexican partner, José Ambriz, had the talent for grouping together dozens of *ejidos* to produce for our American partners, Muranaka Farms.

The unsophisticated *ejido* farmers did not understand the American market. They planted the crops they liked and then tried to find someone to buy them within a very short harvest season. Muranaka Farms proposed finding out what crops major store chains wanted and when. Then the *ejido* could plant with confidence that they had already sold what they grew. Muranaka Farms supplied the money for fertilizers that suited the crops on particular farms. I still recall how Jerry and I dug up plastic bags of soil on some farms for scientific analysis in Los Angeles. Tractors taken down to the Mexicali region plowed the fields and gave them an incline measured by laser beams so that the irrigation water would flow into the ground according to the needs of a particular crop. The entire process was scientific, and crops were planted according to a market analysis of just how much of each crop was needed during a given week of the winter season.

Our agreement called for the American company to pay for schooling of the *ejido* farmers in order to make them self-sufficient in time. When the huge enterprise started to produce a profit, Muranaka Farms canceled the contract with us. We did not have the money to hire lawyers for a long and expensive lawsuit with a multimillion-dollar company, and so we had to just walk away from a business that would assure a secure retirement income for Jerry, Ambriz, and me. Out of desperation, the *ejidos* continued to cooperate with Muranaka Farms. We could understand this, but the loss still hurts me whenever I think of it.

During the presidency of Carlos Salinas de Gortari, the Mexican government decided to privatize the *ejidos* in Mexico. This meant that the families in an *ejido* could acquire full title to their own lands within the former *ejido.* These new property owners were now on their own, however. They could buy, borrow against, rent, or sell their property on which they now paid property taxes. Before long, the new owners started to lose their land by mismanagement because they were generally not prepared to work within the free market system. The paternalistic ideals of the Mexican Revolution were now expressed in a new way that was supposed to create great opportunities. The new policy was called neoliberalism. However, the new freedom turned out to be the freedom of the jungle. Jerry and I gained much gratitude for the help we gave *ejidos* over the years, so we have standing offers of large tracts just about anywhere on the peninsula. Whenever I figure out what to do with the land, I may take up an offer. I am a good historian, but I am not a good businessman.

Chapter 29

SELLING TORTILLAS TO CHINA

I have always felt that you should seize the opportunity to do something extraordinary whenever the chance appeared. This is how I found myself walking along the Great Wall of China in 1993. A Mexican-American acquaintance introduced me to some Chinese businessmen visiting Los Angeles. The visitors were in Los Angeles to promote business, with the help of the Latin Business Association (LBA). Because the Chinese felt discrimination by other Americans, they felt at home with Mexican Americans and wanted to establish warm relations with us. I found this Chinese thinking to be curious, but no less so than the interest of the LBA in doing business in China.

The visitors were here to follow up a visit by the governor of Jilin Province some months before. The LBA hosted the governor and discussed business opportunities. During a visit to the Mexican origins of Los Angeles on Olvera Street, a large party enjoyed Mexican food. It turns out northern Chinese like spicy food, and the governor devoured the enchiladas, rice, and beans. The tamales aroused his interest as did the corn tortillas, which he was taught to tear into pieces to scoop up food like country folk in Mexico. As a man of peasant origins, he admitted pieces of tortilla were easier to use than chopsticks. He was amazed to learn this food was basically made of corn. In China, corn is in surplus but is used only as feed for cattle. Using surplus corn as food for people fascinated the visitors.

The Chinese invited a delegation of the Latin Business Association to visit Jilin Province, and the association warmly accepted the invitation. I tagged along with the LBA group because my idea of a film documentary on China was appealing to the group. I figured that in view of growing trade with the most populous nation, the American public should know more about the Chinese in the interior and not just those living in the huge coastal cities.

It's a long nonstop flight to Tokyo on the way to Beijing. From Tokyo, our group took a beautiful Air China plane to the mainland. I was paying my own expenses and took a video camera to scout for the film documentary on this remote part of the country. China was very much in the news, as trade with this huge communist nation developed and Americans pondered how to relate to this giant communist power.

Beijing was bitterly cold, and we were soon on a regional airplane to Chanchung, the capital of Jilin Province farther north. It was even colder there, close to Russian Siberia. Bilingual Li Gouliang met us, and thank goodness for it. No one else spoke English, and most people just stared at us as we did at them.

The provincial governor had two black limousines for his use. These were the only such cars in northern China. One of these took us from the airport to the grandest hotel I had ever seen. This hotel was reserved for diplomatic visitors and high national government officials. All this was make-believe. Oddly enough, Li always introduced me as Mister Ambassador, and this worked wonders in getting more respect than I deserved. I asked him to introduce me as Professor Nava, but he insisted that in China, titles are very important. It helped us and him that the Chinese saw me as an American ambassador.

After meetings with the governor and other officials, everyone got down to business dealings while I toured the city. The most important business was contracting to import the first of ten tortilla-making machines to Chanchung. It turned out that this province produces as much corn as our American Midwest, and now Mexican tortillas would be made for sale to a population of one and a quarter billion people. That's a lot of tortillas.

I saw enough to convince me that a fascinating documentary could be made on this little-known part of China. At one huge indoor market, we saw the sort of changes that would interest the American television viewer. Outside the market, it was so cold you could not feel your earlobes or the tip of your nose. Inside, there were oranges, watermelons, tomatoes, and all the fresh fruits you could desire, as well as cheese, meat, and the rest. All these summer crops were brought up by train from southern China, which is subtropical. In winter, this southern region of China was no colder than Florida or Southern California. Trains, not roads, hold China together.

The volume of goods came from farmers who produced for the free market. The Chinese government was progressively breaking up the communist collective farms and granting land to individual Chinese families, who could now produce what they wanted and had two choices to sell their produce. The local government agency paid a low price but was a reliable buyer. Farmers could take their chances and sell on the open market at a better price. Free enterprise was thriving in China, and some humble Chinese farmers were accumulating capital for the first time.

The next summer, I returned alone with a better camera and a good idea of what to film. That is how I found myself on a hot summer day climbing along the Great Wall, feeling more at home than before. At a high spot, you can see the wall wind up and down mountains like a snake until it disappears into the horizon. You must be very careful on the Great Wall because the steps are of uneven depth and height. It's not bad climbing up, but very tricky going down.

Li Gouliang and his partner had signed a production contract with three of us in Los Angeles. By this agreement, we would produce the film at our expense, while the Chinese partners would cover our costs in China during the filming. By now, the provincial governor had approved permission for my documentary and the national Ministry of Foreign Affairs had supported the project. When I thought about it, such a green light was quite a distinction.

I traveled by train from Beijing to Chanchung this time and saw much of the country along the way. The railroad station in Beijing was truly something to see. About 10,000 people were camped out on the ground, hoping to buy a ticket for trains that were always sold out. Seats were always oversold even in first-class cars, so my Chinese friend asked me to just hang on to my bags and follow him as he pushed through the crowd like a football player. I was amazed no fights broke out as a mass of people pushed their way through gates to the train. I learned that massive crowds like this waited day and night hoping to get a ride.

During two weeks I traveled all over the province. A bilingual assistant made it possible to communicate with people who were fascinated to meet their first American. In the evening after photography, I would wander out by myself, taking care to mark my route with landmarks to avoid getting lost. I enjoyed seeing and smelling countless small stalls where people prepared food on the sidewalks. I simply pointed and nice ladies served up strange things that tasted delicious. Some of my best footage was at night of such scenes with natural light from stoves burning charcoal. I should not have told Pat about one adventure in Chinese food. Pat has never forgiven me for eating barbecued dog. I didn't know it was dog; it just looked good and tasted better.

I decided to focus the documentary on the everyday life of five Chinese families. The first was a family of farmers now turned businessmen in partnership with former commune members. This group now operated a small hotel, a beer factory, and a processing plant for scrap metal. The group built its own comfortable housing complex and operated its own school for the children. Everyone was very happy and improving their lives day by day. The second family lived modestly from the father's work as a high school teacher. The third family had a father who was a brilliant researcher in optics. He said that only about a dozen individuals in the world could talk to each other in his field of research. I liked the housewife of the fourth family. She was a forewoman in a foundry that made engine blocks for large trucks. She was small and delicate, except for when she shouted orders at the crew in the hot and dangerous foundry. The fifth family was also headed by a woman whose husband worked most of the year in Hungary. This lady was very intelligent and charming as well. She and her parents had suffered greatly during the cultural revolution devised by Chairman Mao Tse-Tung. For years, all her family was punished because her father had operated a small store. The family spent years on their knees crushing stones for roadbeds. Her parents died soon after they were freed, but not before this young lady had learned some of her mother's recipes. From her father she had learned the virtues of being in business for yourself. With the profits from selling fried chicken on sidewalks, she opened a small stall, and then one and then another restaurant. When I filmed her everyday life, she managed her own four-story building full of stores. She was a millionaire in dollars.

Perhaps the sixth family was the most memorable. Purely by chance, one of my Chinese partners was able to introduce me to a remarkable old lady who was a retired librarian. In a former life, she had been the number-one concubine of the last emperor of China. What was hopefully a brief photo encounter turned into two days of conversation and photography that no one else has captured to date. In order to maintain a private life, until then she had not permitted anyone to photograph her.

Mrs. Li was married and lived in modest but comfortable retirement. When the last emperor was overthrown by the communists, the victors did not harm her. Everyone knew that as a pretty peasant girl she had been given to the emperor by the Japanese military commander occupying northern China. Even though we could not communicate, and the translations were simple, she and I liked each other from the start. Perhaps the most surprising footage is of her family gathered on a Sunday afternoon to sip tea, converse, and sing. Group singing is a custom. After some beautiful Chinese folk songs, they broke out with "Old Susannah, Oh don't you cry for me," in Chinese. Someday I will complete this documentary, because I fell in love with China, and the good people there deserve a finished product.

Chapter 30

THE LOS ANGELES MUSIC AND ARTS SCHOOL

Managing the Los Angeles Music and Arts School was one of the most interesting projects I undertook after returning from the embassy in Mexico. The experience reinforced my feeling about the unused talent among our children. It also showed how even well-meaning people can frustrate the hopes of children.

This private school was founded by eastside Jewish folks who wanted to develop artistic talents among children in the neighborhood. When founded over fifty years ago, the group was able to seize this prestigious title because Los Angeles was not very active in the arts. Mostly poor children from East Los Angeles paid a very small tuition to take classes after school. When I accepted the offer to direct the school, children came from all over the city, sometimes in fine cars. The school had a new building, excellent facilities, and very good teachers. The Jewish founders now lived in Beverly Hills, but supported the school out of love for where they had grown up.

One particular episode at the school is worth telling about. Rubén Zacarías, who later became superintendent of the Los Angeles Unified School District, was then superintendent of Area G, one of nine subdivisions of the school district. We shaped a plan whereby each of the ninety-two elementary schools in Rubén's area would have a painting contest for sixth-graders on the theme of "L.A., My Hometown." In a month, the paintings made up a tall stack on the floor. My governing board would not pay for any costs because they felt the school district should do it. I gained some contributions and the free services of two professional artists as judges. *La Opinión,* the largest Spanish-language newspaper, agreed to give prizes and publish color photographs of the best works. On one Sunday, several hundred family members appeared to watch the winning children get awards and their first-ever diplomas.

The sixth-graders had not graduated from elementary school yet, and so the ceremony was most impressive for them. Each winner walked down the long aisle in his or her Sunday-best outfit, with smiling relatives looking on. Each was given a diploma and had a picture taken as everyone clapped. I am sure these children will never forget the experience.

After the long and tiring ceremony, one of the painters and I were conversing. He had learned that I liked to paint and did whenever I could. As a challenge, he asked me to pick out the ten best of the winning paintings. He said there was some hope for my painting as hobby, but I should never try to earn a living painting. I had picked only four of the ten best paintings out of the ninety.

After explaining why he made his choices, he stopped short and gasped. "Julian," he said, "of these ten best, two or three show great promise, maybe four." We then both spoke out at the same time in excitement. The students in Area G schools were about 90 percent Mexican American. Next year there would be another sixth-grade class, and so forth the year after. And this was only one of nine regions in the entire school district (which is 65 percent Spanish-surname now). In a few years we could have a painting renaissance in Los Angeles, if these children could get instruction in painting in later grades, I observed. He corrected me. "You should not teach them how to paint, only help them develop what talent they already have."

We left the paintings hanging for a while. At a fundraiser, Bob Hope was impressed by the children's work, as were other celebrities. The school was moving along very well, so I wanted to expand its operations in ways that unexpectedly caused a rift with the board. This rift led to my departure after just two years.

I had made arrangements for our choir and musicians to start a series of performances at the Los Angeles County Jail. Most of the inmates were Mexican Americans and blacks and not serious offenders. I guessed that watching children perform would make these folks rethink their conduct and return to their home and children with another view of life. The county jail staff was enthusiastic about the project. The students and the jail were ready, but some board members objected to the association of the school with the county jail.

At Pomona College, classical music was something everyone studied, and all my friends at Harvard loved fine music also. Because we were always broke, we would gather in someone's room and listen to the Boston Symphony perform all Sunday afternoon. I can still recall arguments over who directed Beethoven's Seventh Symphony better, Toscanini or Karl Munche. All this helps explain my love for good music and the delightful assignment to run a music and art school.

A friend of mine had organized La Sinfónica del Barrio, a neighborhood symphony orchestra of volunteers. Their performances were fair, and now and then they did very well. Director Pete Quezada desperately needed a place for rehearsals, and I offered the large hall of our school at no cost. I figured that our prestige would benefit as the home of this unique orchestra. Some of our students could grow with the experience of playing with adults in a symphony orchestra.

Once again I had trouble with the board, who felt the orchestra should pay rent for our facility. This project was aborted also, and before long I left the directorship by mutual consent. My revenge was to become president of the board of trustees of La Sinfónica del Barrio, which has limped along for over ten years. It was sad to observe during fundraising efforts that benefactors tend to help minority groups in sports, but not when they play in symphony orchestras or other sophisticated endeavors.

The directorship experience only reinforced my conviction that we have an enormous pool of talent among our young people, and they need only a chance to get started. As demography moves Mexican-American and other Hispanic youths into the overwhelming majority in our public schools, our society will need more than just athletes from these beautiful brown children. I look back at this experience with the Los Angeles Music and Art School as a failure on my part because I did not know how to deal with a complicated situation of the well-meaning traditional board of governors, on the one hand, and changing conditions in our community, on the other.

Chapter 31

Nava for Mayor of Los Angeles

I decided to run for mayor of Los Angeles in 1993, against my better judgment. Numerous friends had encouraged me to reenter politics because they claimed we needed more people in leadership positions. I had resisted the idea so far. This mayoral race is interesting as a commentary on Mexican-American politics in the 1990s.

It all started in an indirect manner. Several friends drew me into discussions about East Los Angeles Community College, where we all had graduated. We were concerned about the explosive increase in enrollment, on the one hand, and the lack of resources to support the educational programs, on the other. The community college board was bleeding the college, to make matters worse. State income for each college is based on enrollment. Several community colleges in white, middle-class parts of the city had a declining enrollment, largely due to smaller family size. The costs of those campuses were constant because the salaries and maintenance remained the same, even if there were fewer students attending. Money due to "East L.A.," as we called it, was diverted to the other colleges for numerous years, and this explained the physical and educational decline of our beloved college. What the trustees were doing was legal although unfair, we believed.

A group of graduates started meeting at La Carreta, one

of the best Mexican-food joints in East L.A. It was a political watering hole. You still find politicians eating there at all hours. At these early breakfast meetings, about twenty of us came up with the idea of fixing up the college with help from community groups. We figured that we could enlist hundreds of skilled volunteers to work on weekends. Over several weeks we established a list of physical repairs needed at the campus. Because the committee included folks in many walks of life and with broad connections, we set out to recruit people in painting, gardening, construction, and so forth. Most of the local businesspeople were alumni. In order to broaden support, we got about ten Mexican-American-elected officials to send a personal representative to the breakfast meetings. These lasted one hour only so all could be at work on time. For me, it meant leaving home at six to beat the morning freeway traffic.

The group presented our plan to the central college system trustees to get their approval, and I was asked to speak for the group. The trustees understood that we were doing this community organizing because of their policy of bleeding our college resources. In spite of this, the trustees thought our idea was very creative and a model for the entire district of six colleges to follow.

Later in 1992, it became clear that Los Angeles Mayor Thomas Bradley would not run for reelection. His first two terms were successful, and Tom became one of the nation's most prominent black public figures. Now, following an explosive citywide riot on the heels of the Rodney King police beating trial, his reputation was tarnished and he was tired. Over hot tortillas with scrambled eggs and beans, our East L.A. community college group concluded that the mechanism we had built up to help the college could serve to launch a Chicano candidate for mayor. The college committee was thus diverted from Saturday gardening efforts at the campus. All the men and women in our committee were seasoned political activists, and so the group reorganized into a political action committee. Subcommittees went to work contacting every viable Chicano public figure who might run for mayor, starting with officeholders. One by one, it became clear that people in Congress, state senators, state assembly members, city council members, and a county supervisor were not going to run for mayor in Los Angeles. Gloria Molina, a member of the county board of supervisors, was the last holdout because she had hoped for a position in newly-elected President Bill Clinton's cabinet.

I spoke with Gloria in her luxurious supervisor offices. We knew each other well. When she ran for state assembly for the first time, against Richard Polanco, another friend of mine, I gave her my public support. As a school board member elected at large in Los Angeles County, my endorsement was helpful, since my electoral district contained ten members of Congress. She gained election over the favorite, Richard, and it took a long time for him to forgive me, if he ever did. (Richard was later elected to the state legislature and became a statewide political power broker and creative policy-thinker.)

Gloria stated that she was not a candidate, although her door was slightly open to the possibility. In the event she did not run for mayor, she made it clear that she would not endorse anyone else, however. By now the breakfast group had made substantial progress in getting many community groups involved in the race for mayor. The idea was to identify a citywide candidate with unified support. Gloria was the most powerful Chicano elected official at this time, and the committee believed her support for the consensus candidate was vital. By now her representative at the La Carreta meetings informed her that some committee members thought I should run for mayor if no Chicano officeholder did. As it turned out, Gloria would not return the favor of my early endorsement of her.

The race for mayor in 1993 was important. It was our chance to elect a Mexican-American mayor. Tom Bradley probably would have gotten elected again had he decided to run, chiefly because of political inertia. White people voted for Bradley, as did all blacks and most other minorities. Mexican-American leaders and voters supported him every time he ran for mayor, as well as for governor of California. Given this history, and Bradley's decision not to seek another term, our committee assumed that blacks would support a Mexican American this time around. This was the first of several false assumptions we made.

In 1993, a Mexican American had a real chance to become mayor of what was becoming a Mexican-American city. Of the city's population of 3.2 million at that time, Spanish-surnamed residents made up 41 percent. Mayor Bradley had helped his people in practical ways and as a role model during twenty years in office. He also demonstrated that a black official could serve everyone, regardless of race. This open seat was an historic opportunity for Mexican Americans to do the same thing. The committee felt that we should not let the opportunity pass by.

Only after every Mexican-American officeholder declined to be a candidate, or would not answer the question put to them, did the organizing committee convince me to run. As one friend put it, the Chicano community of Los Angeles would look pitiful if no one rose to seize an historic opportunity that might not come again for a long time, if ever.

Pat's opinion was simple: "If you win, then I'll wish you good luck and good-bye." Pat had had enough of public life after the ambassadorial experience. This shocked me, but I assured her that I would not win, but would run a good race. This effort would help the image of Mexican Americans while providing an opportunity to talk plainly to the people of Los Angeles about issues that viable candidates tend to avoid for fear of losing votes.

The planning committee acquired a copy of a poll taken by another candidate that revealed that 37 percent of those asked recognized the name Nava. This name recognition was among the best of the other major candidates and offered hope that I could emerge among the top two candidates in the primary. With a vigorous voter registration drive among the fast-growing Mexican-American population, the basic ingredients for making it to the runoff elections were present, it seemed.

Before long, a remarkable twenty-four individuals filed papers to run for mayor. This number was a record. While this seemed like a disadvantage, it helped the Nava campaign because the high number of candidates would split the votes so much that it could be easier to be one of the two highest vote-getters and then appear in the runoff election. Mayor Bradley, to his credit, promised not to support any candidate, including the two candidates who were black. Our committee spoke to some black leaders about discouraging competing black candidates, but they just stared back in surprise that we would ask for a return of the favor.

Other serious problems emerged after the Nava campaign was launched with a press conference on the steps of City Hall. Each of these problems was enough to doom an effort that initially appeared to have much promise. Some of these problems were internal to our Hispanic community and others came from the outside.

A wealthy Irish Catholic businessman decided to run. Richard Riordan claimed to have a personal fortune of $100 million and said he was ready to spend $6 million of it to fund his campaign. No other candidate could compete with that much money. The amount threatened to purchase the election. Besides being unknown to the public, he had another problem. As a Catholic, he could not get a divorce, so he was living with another woman who was his true love. To the city's credit, no one brought up this situation. His financial commitment was devastating, however. Many possible contributors held back because the results seemed determined.

The two black candidates claimed the black voters, even though Hispanics had always supported black candidates in order to form a common cause for minorities. Blacks wanted another black mayor, no matter what. In view of the population growth of the Spanish-surnamed, many blacks felt endangered and believed that it was all the more important to "stop the Mexicans."

Others felt the same way. Our Brain Trust campaign committee suspected a conspiracy to stop me when four totally unknown Mexican Americans appeared on the ballot. By simply having their names appear on the ballot, each could obtain 3 to 5 percent of the votes. It was safe to assume that most of these votes would have gone to me.

In addition to these surprise candidates, restaurant owner Linda Griego proved to be the most damaging. Mayor Bradley had appointed Griego as one of several deputy mayors, which gave her some name recognition. Linda received substantial monetary support from a national group supporting women candidates across the country. She had few relationships with local Hispanic community groups, but her campaign publicity helped her gain female voters as the only woman candidate.

The other Hispanic candidates rarely appeared in public, although Griego did now and then. At one candidates' forum in the barrio, I asked her to explain why she was running and contributing to a split in the Hispanic vote. She would not say anything directly, except that anyone should be free to run for public office. Soon after his election, Mayor Riordan appointed her to head the multimillion-dollar "Rebuild L.A." program. Almost nothing came from this effort, but for Riordan's first term, she was on a very good salary and gained membership in a prestigious corporation's board of trustees. No one ever heard of the other Hispanic candidates after the elections. They just disappeared. Splitting the votes of your opponent has been a continuing practice in American politics, and it has sunk many Hispanic campaigns before. It surely doomed this campaign.

The Chinese-American candidate, Los Angeles council member Michael Woo, split the Hispanic vote in another manner. Woo narrowly won the endorsement of the Mexican-American Political Association. Ironically, MAPA was established in order to support Mexican-American candidates and support causes beneficial to them. I was among the earliest members of MAPA in the late 1940s, but MAPA had lost much ground in recent years.

An old friend of our family, Bert Corona, was among its founders and now operated a community service group to help immigrants from Mexico, where he was born. Immigrants received help at this center with welfare, jobs, and lessons for citizenship. Bert was at the endorsing convention, which seemed like a good thing because he was regarded as an elder statesman of Chicano public life.

While I was speaking to the large audience, I noticed that a large bloc of men sitting in the center remained passive. Others reacted to my animated remarks, but these hundred or so just sat there. I realized, as I spoke in English, that they could not understand me. After the vote, Woo got the endorsement of MAPA to everyone's surprise except Corona. As it turned out, the federally funded agency directed by Corona to help immigrants had bused them to the convention and paid their entrance fee. Michael Woo had made a large contribution to Corona's agency, and so Corona delivered the votes to endorse Woo for mayor. Al Juárez, who worked for Mayor Bradley, and now for Woo, told my brother Henry how this happened, and said to him, "You must understand, Hank, this is only business."

The crowning blow to the Nava campaign for mayor was that not a single Mexican-American-elected official supported the campaign. This was amazing because I knew virtually all these folks. Our campaign Brain Trust had reported one case after another where the officeholders wanted to sit on the fence. Los Angeles City Councilman Mike Hernández put it bluntly after a group of us finally got to speak to him. "Julian," he said, "I am going with the winner." The other prominent Chicano councilman, Richard Alatorre, was bought off by Riordan with the promise of an appointment to the prestigious MTA, the Metropolitian Transit Authority.

And so it went. Riordan and Woo were in the finals, and Riordan got elected on the strength of a simple slogan heard and seen constantly in all the media: "Riordan. Strong enough to turn L.A. around." The city's second major race riot in twenty-five years had most voters focused on issues of public safety.

I expressed many good ideas during countless community forums and debates with other candidates. Most of the rivals developed a friendship with me and mutual respect. Two others would have made very good mayors, and I said so more than once, much to their surprise. Griego, Woo, and Riordan rarely attended these public forums, relying mainly on their paid advertisements. The other major candidates complained about these absences, but there was nothing to be done.

The absence of a united front on the part of Hispanic

officeholders was impressive to Hispanics, and I believe to outsiders as well. It demonstrated a blend of weakness, lack of maturity, and timidity among leadership in this ever more numerous part of the community.

The Nava campaign did enjoy the doomed effort in some ways. Aside from clarifying who your friends really were, and finding many new ones, there were some interesting episodes. Early in the campaign, Riordan invited me to his home for an early and private breakfast. He proudly showed me the enlargement of his house and a huge library with many rare books. I joked with him that these books ought to be in a university library and not on his cellar shelves. I guessed that during our pleasant conversation and backslapping he might be looking where to place a knife. I felt guilty about the suspicion, but later events supported my early belief that this fellow would do anything to get what he wanted. Acting friendly did not cost him much.

My files on the campaign have been deposited in the Urban Archives at Cal State Northridge for researchers who care to understand what happened. Still today, I regret the loss of a major opportunity for the Hispanic community to evolve and lead in America's second-largest city.

Chapter 32

My Trip to Siberia

One of my son's friends, Bert Nuranen, was a public school teacher home for Christmas from his temporary assignment teaching English to high school students in Novosibirsk (New Siberia). One thing led to another over coffee, and before long we had devised a filming project in Siberia.

Bert took copies of my Basque and Cuba documentaries to Siberia and showed them to the director of the National Institute on Anthropology. He hinted that perhaps I would be willing to film a documentary on Siberia today. I was actually anxious to do it, but I was playing hard to get. The director at the institute liked my work, and within a month I received a formal invitation to visit in order to explore the possibility of a documentary. They were very anxious for me to do the job as long as I funded the project. The institute was broke. Their salaries, like those all over the Russian Federation, were six months behind schedule. The Russians promised all sorts of on-site cooperation and access to materials. This would be financial support, in effect.

I chose to leave immediately because, due to a strike at American Airlines, all the other carriers dropped their prices in half to compete with strike-inspired fare reductions at American. I bought my tickets on the last day of the cut-rate fares and before I could obtain funding from any foundation or group. Poor Pat, she is a good trooper, and simply asked, "Where are you going this time? Siberia in winter! Are you nuts?"

All you could see was white as the airliner dropped down close to Moscow. No one spoke English, nor were there any signs in English as there always are in Europe. I was getting anxious because I could not spot a man with a red scarf who was supposed to meet me coming out of customs. After a short time with growing anxiety, I walked up to a man waiting for incoming travelers, even if he was not wearing a red scarf, and sure enough, it was the right fellow. After a very simple lunch in a rather worn-down restaurant, he took me by bus to another airport on the opposite side of the city. I would never have made it alone. It turns out that Moscow has several airports scattered about for military defense reasons. After pointing out the exact door for me to enter eight hours later, I insisted that he go back to work while I waited. The flights to Novosibirsk from Moscow are all at night. This domestic airport was run down and not very clean.

What a boring wait until my flight left for Siberia. I napped, holding on to my bags because I had been warned about thieves. I had heard about poor maintenance on Areoflot, the domestic government airline. Sure enough, the plane was rather bare with none of the comfortable things you find on Western airlines. My concern was not taking off, but rather landing in the dark. The runways were snow-covered, and I figured the pilots must make a perfect landing or skid off the runway. I was one of only fifteen passengers on this huge aircraft. The midnight meal was simple but good, and after a long nap, we landed perfectly in the dark at a frozen airport serving Novosibirsk. The airport was far away from the city for military reasons, I learned.

What a relief to see my American friend and Ola with

him. Ola was charming and never stopped talking. As assistant to the director of the Russian Institute of Anthropology, she was super-efficient. Best of all, she spoke English. Later in the week, Nuranen and I had supper with her parents and Ola's beautiful ten-year-old daughter. Ola's mother was built like a tank and was a much-decorated battle heroine of the Second World War. A wartime photograph of her showed a chestful of medals. Her father was a researcher in a field I still do not understand. He was so highly regarded that the government had allotted him a large home on an acre with beautiful trees. The family relied on their vegetable garden for food, however.

I stayed with my Granada Hills High School teacher, sleeping on a narrow couch in the kitchen. The Russian refrigerator made so much noise that it awakened me every time it turned on during the night. At last I pulled the plug until morning, since nothing was about to thaw, anyway. All the chairs and couches in the living room were designed to torture you. We cooked the most basic foods, but not much, because Nuranen was under doctor's orders to lose weight. Since I don't like to cook, I suffered with his diet.

The place where we lived demonstrated recent Russian history. We were in a small apartment in a huge apartment complex, just like many buildings in the suburb around us. This small city was called Academ Gorodok, or Academic City. Located about 20 miles from Novosibirsk (again, for military reasons), it was built very quickly during the time of Nikita Khrushchev as a self-sufficient city for advanced scholars and researchers in science. About 15,000 of Russia's best minds lived here and worked on government projects. The most advanced researchers, like Ola's father, lived in a comfortable house with land to grow food, and not in the huge apartment buildings.

To visit Academ Gorodok, you passed through a security checkpoint, although probably it was no longer needed after the Cold War. The breakdown of the communist Soviet Union created economic chaos everywhere. Government tax revenues dropped, and one after another public agency could not pay salaries. Professors in Academ Gorodok had not been paid for three months when I was there. Government employees and other workers were selling personal possessions to eat, and suicides were increasing. Widows were paid pensions more faithfully than retirees, so a number of suicides were attributed to men providing for their wives. It was so cold in Siberia that my camera caught a cold, so to speak. Sometimes it would film only in black and white, but when I warmed it under my parka, it would film in color, until it got cold again.

With the authority of her director, Ola arranged meetings with groups and individuals who promised to help me when I returned the next summer to film from the Ural Mountains to Vladivostok on the Pacific Ocean coast. This region is so large that the United States would fit into it one-and-a-half times. The resources there are enormous and varied. People there resent Moscow and feel like a group apart.

On the last night, a group of us went to the ballet in Novosibirsk in a jammed public bus. Like everyone else, I pushed my way in and got the front seat alongside the driver. In the back with the other sardines, I would have become very anxious on the long ride sliding down the icy road. The huge city is not beautiful because all the buildings are alike, having been built very quickly. The city was built under communism to safely house factories and researchers far away from bombers that would come from western Europe. The opera house was the one beautiful building in Novosibirsk. It reminded me of a beautiful palace built under the Russian czars, when money and cheap labor were plentiful. In this case, several thousand German prisoners of war built this temple to the arts. In fact, Adolf Hitler's soldiers worked themselves to death to build this monument to culture. When I asked about this, no one expressed any remorse. I felt somber about this until I remembered that the German invasion during the Second World War cost more than ten million Russian lives.

Among the impressions that struck me were the large number of children in the audience and how reverent everyone was of the performance. You would think you were in church. The orchestra and the ballet were superb in the middle of frozen Siberia. I did not sleep after the opera because the flight back to Moscow left at 4 A.M. I left a piece of my heart behind when I hugged Ola and slid on the ice toward the plane. One way or another, I will produce a documentary on what I call the new Siberia. Americans have an opportunity to help shape a new life for these wonderful people halfway around the world. A better life for Siberians protects ours.

During the visit, I helped Bert establish student body government in the high school in Academ Gorodok as a pilot program. Bert and I believed that this project could have long-range influences in the Russian Federation. The stern principal was suspicious of this experiment, but most teachers were willing to give the American idea a chance. Bert had taken along a copy of the student body constitution from Abraham Lincoln High School in East Los Angeles. Bert had been teaching there during the famous walkouts of 1968. Bert got the constitution translated into Russian for the students to consider as a model. I filmed students electing their first student body officers and shaping a constitution modeled on the one formed by Chicano students in Los Angeles.

The first action the student body council took was to propose a dance. The principal's opposition to the proposal was overcome when student officers argued that such new activities would be good for school morale and promote a spirit of cooperation with the administration. How quickly the students applied persuasion in the new political arena. By now the school has probably set an example for other high schools in Novosibirsk, and maybe beyond. Students do not enjoy the right to have self-government in the Russian Federation so far, and so Bert's project may be a historic trendsetter for all of Russia.

Chapter 33

Teaching at My Alma Mater

Pomona College gave me an honorary doctor's degree after I returned from Mexico, as did Whittier College. I was also invited to join the board of trustees of Pomona. I was thrilled by this invitation to work with such splendid individuals in guiding my alma mater, one of the best small liberal arts colleges in the nation.

I was asked to give a course on relations between the United States and Mexico from my perspective as ambassador there. I prepared especially detailed lectures and gave the students a lot of information not commonly found in books. Now and then during a lecture, I would be surprised hearing myself lecture in a classroom where I had been a student.

Relations between students and their professors continue to be casual at Pomona, and so I would arrive early for the evening class. I ate at the huge and impressive Frary Hall Dining Room, where my students gathered for good conversation over the meal. Over us at the end of the hall we could enjoy the world-famous mural of Prometheus, by the great Mexican muralist Orozco. My office was used by my former professor Jack Kemble, who had retired and then passed away. Working in Professor Kemble's office was an emotional experience. I recalled incidents with him fifty years earlier. Sometimes I would sit at his desk and ponder that he still seemed to be in the room. I hope some of my students recall me with fondness.

I telephoned the department chairman for help after reading the term papers and final exams. He burst out laughing when I explained my problem. Only one student had earned a B grade; all the rest were A or A-plus. I told him this was awkward and defied all laws of averages. He was still chuckling when he said students at Pomona today might be better than when I graduated in 1951. I agreed, even though our Class of '51 was by reputation one of Pomona's best.

Chapter 34

FACING THE END OF MY JOURNEY

A few months ago my very good childhood friend José Castorena died alone of a heart attack while working in his office one Saturday morning. His cleaning woman found him on Monday. The loss of such a close friend made a big impression on me. I still have the funeral windshield sticker "Funeral" pinned up in my office.

Joe and I would argue much of the time, driving from one end of Mexico to the other with our mutual friend Gonzalo Molina. Gonzalo had a photographic memory about Mexican history. His father was a major figure in the shaping of the Mexican Constitution of 1917, and Gonzalo was a dedicated politician. He ran for public office over and over, but losing never discouraged him. The three of us argued all day long about the places we were passing and then enjoyed a good dinner and Mexican beer before we retired early. Others might say we were arguing, but we just enjoyed intense discussions. We were like the characters in the "Odd Couple" movies. One argument was real; it had to do with getting up at 5:30 A.M. Joe insisted we hit the road at seven.

Another dear friend, Morrie Coldwell, learned that he would soon die from bone marrow cancer. My first reaction was anger when he phoned. How could he do this to us? We were fishing buddies and enjoyed endless conversations about education, politics, and everything else. Morrie, an Irishman, was married to a Jewish woman for so many years that he was practically Jewish. He made me laugh with all the jokes Jews make of themselves. "Do you know what a 'schmuck' is?" he would ask. "That's a guy who picks a nickel over a dime because it's larger," he would answer himself. Since he was confined to bed, I visited him almost daily until he died.

My older sister Lucy died recently, and I still cannot get used to not seeing her again. She was a role model for me: always caring, patient, and helpful to everyone. She was an ideal minister's wife. My younger sister Rosemarie just lost her husband, also to a heart attack. We were regular Monday-night football fans, as well as friends. All these losses have made me sad, but only more resolved to live life fully.

Everything takes a little longer now, I notice. My cousin Miguel Flores and I have prepared a video on the history of Zacatecas, where both our families hail from. It will be the first documentary on this vital state of Mexico. In the middle of this, Miguel talked me into helping raise funds for a monument to Dámaso Muñatones, a native of Zacatecas and one of Mexico's great architects of colonial-style churches. Meanwhile, my proposal for a documentary on Iran has been approved by the president and the ayatollah there. It's hard to believe but true. The Mexican consul general in Los Angeles has agreed to help with my production of a documentary for schools on the Cinco de Mayo. If it's a good job, and it should be, schools across the country will know more about Mexico. This will help others to better understand the ever-growing number of Mexican-American children from one coast to the other. I must try harder to overcome one personal fault. I have many interests and start to do too many things at once.

My nephew Vern is visiting us from Alaska, where several of our nephews now live. He said in response to my question about undocumented Mexican workers, "Uncle, they are all over the place, especially the fishing industry out on the Eleutian Island chain that points towards Russian Siberia. The INS rounds them up now and then, but others soon take their place." It is ironic that these Mexican workers have returned to the route and location where their ancestors came from many thousands of years before.

Pat and I have moved also. We sold our home close to the college campus where I started teaching in 1957 in order to follow our three children and four grandchildren to Escondido, just north of San Diego. We now live on a five-acre ranch on a high summit covered with oak trees and rolling hills that give us a beautiful sunset every day. We are happy with the grandchildren running around and making a mess at Grandma's and playing with Grandpa's computer. This is as far as I will go. I am home.

Excellent health makes me feel like fifty-three instead of seventy-three years old. As a boy in the barrio, I did not imagine seeing the year 2000, but here I am. The Nava clan and friends just celebrated my sister Helen's 80th birthday with a huge *pachanga,* and since she deliberately danced with all the men to lively mariachi music, I feel like my journey has a way to go. I am still running, although a little slower.

Additional titles in our
Hispanic Civil Rights Series

Message to Aztlán
Rodolfo "Corky" Gonzales
ISBN 1-55885-331-6

A Gringo Manual on How to Handle Mexicans
José Angel Gutiérrez
ISBN 1-55885-326-X

Eyewitness: A Filmmaker's Memoir of the Chicano Movement
Jesús Treviño
ISBN 1-55885-349-9

Pioneros puertorriqueños en Nueva York, 1917–1947
Joaquín Colón
ISBN 1-55885-335-9

The American GI Forum: In Pursuit of the Dream, 1948–1983
Henry Ramos
Clothbound, ISBN 1-55885-261-1
Trade Paperback, ISBN 1-55885-262-X

Chicano! The History of the Mexican American Civil Rights Movement
F. Arturo Rosales
ISBN 1-55885-201-8

Testimonio: A Documentary History of the Mexican-American Struggle for Civil Rights
F. Arturo Rosales
ISBN 1-55885-299-9

They Called Me "King Tiger": My Struggle for the Land and Our Rights
Reies López Tijerina
ISBN 1-55885-302-2

Memoir of a Visionary: Antonia Pantoja
Antonia Pantoja
ISBN 1-55885-385-5

DISCARD
WITHDRAWAL